Also by Klaus Truemper

Brain Science

Artificial Intelligence
Magic, Error, and Terror

History

The Daring Invention of Logarithm Tables
The Construction of Mathematics

Technical

Logic-based Intelligent Systems
Effective Logic Computation
Matroid Theory

Edited by Ingrid and Klaus Truemper

F. Hülster *Introduction to Wittgenstein's*
Tractatus Logico-Philosophicus
(English and German edition)

F. Hülster *Berlin 1945: Surviving the Collapse*

WITTGENSTEIN
AND
BRAIN SCIENCE

UNDERSTANDING
THE WORLD

KLAUS TRUEMPER

Leibniz Company

Softcover published by Leibniz Company
2304 Cliffside Drive
Plano, Texas, 75023
USA

The book is typeset in LATEX using the Tufte-style book class, which was inspired by the work of Edward R. Tufte and Richard Feynman.

Sources and licenses for all figures are listed in the Notes section.

Library of Congress Cataloging-in-Publication Data
Truemper, Klaus, 1942–

Wittgenstein and Brain Science: Understanding the World
ISBN 978-0-9991402-3-9
1. Wittgenstein. 2. Brain. 3. Neuroprocesses.

Contents

1

Introduction

Have you ever wondered why philosophers have debated some questions about the world for centuries? Famous examples include:[1]

- Do we have free will?
- What is the nature of knowledge?
- What is time?

Other people concerned with complex problems—scientists, mathematicians, engineers, economists, psychologists, and so on—also have offered conflicting solutions for difficult problems in their areas. There is a fundamental difference, though. The discussion typically results in some consensus, and people move on.

Why is philosophy different?

Before we can answer that question, we need to consider basic results about reasoning.

Until recently, most everybody assumed that humans could think and reason in a reliable and consistent manner. For example, Plato (c. 424–c. 348 BCE) didn't believe he was confused when he postulated that there is a world of ideas, and René Descartes (1596–1650) was convinced that his arguments about mind and body were correct. The same assumption of certainty extended to situations where a philosopher claimed something to be undecidable or in error; for example, when Agrippa the Skeptic (1st century) declared that we must suspend judgment of validity for most theories, or when David Hume (1711–1776) asserted that other philosophers were mistaken or confused about the substance of the world.

In short, it was assumed that the thinking process was done by a reliable *input/output machine*.[2]

The concept of input/output machine is independent of the location thinking was postulated to take place: whether in the heart, the brain, the mind, or without specified location in the person.[3]

Modern brain science has replaced the concept of input/output machine with a far-ranging theory of reasoning by the *nervous system*, which consists of the *brain*, the *spinal cord*, and the *network of nerves*. The network connects the brain and the spinal cord to the rest of the body, for example, to the eyes, ears, organs, muscles, blood vessels, and glands.[4]

You may be surprised when we say now that some reasoning occurs partially or wholly outside the nervous system and isn't covered by brain science. For example, such reasoning guards the body against harm caused by excessive physical effort, or it selects the optimal pace when we hike in the mountains.[5]

You may wonder how we can claim this. After all, don't we think about protecting the body and selecting the pace? Yes, we do. But how do we know whether a physical effort is damaging the body or a pace isn't optimal? The reasoning processes that answer these questions involve parts of the body outside the nervous system and aren't accessible to conscious inspection. If you want to see details, jump ahead to Chapters 3 and 5.

We need a general definition of the activities in the human body that accommodates these decision processes and more. To this end, we declare any process in the body that involves information acquisition and subsequent reaction in any form, to be a *neuroprocess*.

We use this term knowing full well that some neuroprocesses take place in part or wholly outside the nervous system.

We are aware of some of the neuroprocesses while others escape conscious attention. We call the neuroprocesses we are aware of *conscious*, and the rest *subconscious*.

———————

How do the concepts of mind and intelligence fit into these definitions?

We consider *mind* to be the awareness of the conscious neuroprocesses as they take place. This implies that the mind isn't an entity separate from the body.

We declare that *intelligence* is *demonstrated* by the neuroprocesses when they achieve their goals. The definition is consistent with the usual interpretation where we consider the fact that we speak, drive cars, invent machinery, read books, and fly to the moon to be evidence of intelligence.

The definition also covers other evidence of intelligence, for example, the situations where neuroprocesses protect the body from excessive physical effort and select the optimal pace during a hike.

The definition even declares intelligence to be present at much lower levels of the body, for example, when a neuroprocess is the defensive action of bacteria against invading viruses.[6]

The definition of neuroprocesses doesn't conflict with the correct claim that a person, and not the brain, thinks.[7] After all, the definition of the neuroprocesses implies that they carry out a person's reasoning as well as many other things.

———————

The title of this book includes the popular term "brain science." The technical term is "neuroscience." We need a term that captures not just the traditional definition of brain science—or neuroscience, if you like—but also accommodates all neuroprocesses currently not included. For this, we now expand the definition of "neuroscience" to include those missing neuroprocesses. We drop "brain science" entirely to avoid confusion.

We hope that this expansion of the term "neuroscience" doesn't draw the ire of neuroscientists. It is consistent with the fact that many investigations of neuroscientists, for example using fMRI (functional magnetic resonance imaging), already connect the nervous system with the rest of the body.

Before we go on and look at the use of neuroprocesses in philosophy, we should clarify that the idea of neuroprocesses is not new and can be traced back to the 19th century. Of course, the terminology was different, and definitions were narrower and didn't cover all processes of the body involving information acquisition and subsequent reaction in any form.[8] A key figure in these early developments is Hermann von Helmholtz (1821–1894).[9] For example, he postulated mental processes that convert visual input outside conscious control into conscious images. These processes are instances of the subconscious neuroprocesses defined here.

Let's return to the question why the debates for some philosophical problems do not converge to a commonly accepted solution. Here is our answer.

The root cause is the erroneous viewpoint that reasoning is done as if an input/output machine was used. When instead we consider reasoning based on subconscious and conscious neuroprocesses, in many cases we can

- offer a reasonable common-sense solution, or

- demonstrate that a generally accepted solution cannot be determined at the present time and, in our opinion, will not be established in the foreseeable future.

Regardless of the outcome, we say that we have *resolved* the problem.

The explanation may be surprising, even startling. How is it possible that the implicit assumption of an input/output machine prevents the solution of philosophical problems, while the consideration of neuroprocesses brings clarity? We do not have a short answer and can only promise that the subsequent chapters will supply the explanation.

Let's look at an example. You are on the beach. Somebody asks you, "Do you know where the Oyster Bar is located?" You have been there and can help. Since the walk from the beach to the restaurant is a bit complicated, you draw a map in the wet sand to explain the route. How did you come up with the idea that you can draw lines in wet sand that correspond to streets?

It's difficult to imagine how an input/output machine could produce that idea. So where does it come from?

The philosopher Plato (c. 424–c. 348 BCE) had an answer for this difficult question. He said that there is a world of timeless, absolute, and unchangeable ideas that we do not sense and can only think about. When you draw lines that depict the streets leading to the restaurant, you use concepts of that world of ideas.

Do you really rely on that world, or is something else going on? More generally: Does the world of ideas exist?

Philosophers have debated the latter question since Plato's times. In Chapter 8 we take it up and offer an answer that traces Plato's concept back to the concept of input/output machine and resolves the problem using neuroprocesses.

We use two tools for our investigation.

- A comprehensive format for the conscious and subconscious neuroprocesses. We call it the *neuroprocess hypothesis*.

- An enhanced version of the language games that the philosopher Ludwig Wittgenstein (1889–1951) proposed for understanding philosophical statements. We call that version *reflected language games*.

We resolve a number of long-standing questions. They include the following cases:

- What is the nature of knowledge? (Chapter 12)
- Can we ever prove a theory? (Chapter 15)
- What is time? (Chapter 19)
- What is the substance of the world? (Chapter 20)
- Do we have free will? (Chapter 25)
- Is mathematics part of the world? Is it discovered or invented? (Chapters 9 and 23)

The idea of applying science to philosophy is not new. Time and again, new insight in the sciences impacted philosophy.

For example, the non-Euclidean geometries created by mathematicians in the 19th century destroyed the prior assumption that Euclidean geometry was the unique framework for the universe.[10] A similar change occurred in the 20th century for the concept of time when empirical and theoretical evidence proved that it isn't an independent quantity. Indeed, it is influenced by actions and forces of the universe.[11]

Going back further, the sciences removed angels, devils, Eden, heaven, and hell from the physical universe and sometimes argued that gods are mere bystanders or even nonentities.[12] The world's religions either rejected those conclusions or adapted their claims.

Can the neuroprocess hypothesis and reflected language games do more than resolve philosophical problems? Yes, indeed. Here is an example.

Robots bombard us daily, indeed almost every minute, with information and try to influence our lives. They urge us to purchase something, to think well of or—alternately—to despise some politician, to change our life style, and so on.

The social and news media play a key role in this massive attempt to direct our lives. The tools employed here can help us identify harmful agendas hidden in supposedly benign statements.

In the best-case scenario, the tools eventually bring us to the point where we ignore the flood of manipulative drivel and come back to a simpler life.

———————

Philosophers and scientists have explored the link between neuroscience and philosophy in two ways.

- Philosophers have relied on concepts of their field to examine results of neuroscience.
- Scientists have employed results of neuroscience to investigate philosophical claims.

The work in either direction is so extensive that we couldn't possibly include a summary.[13] Suffice it to say that this book is part of the second effort.

A technical comment: The Notes section contains additional explanations and discussions. During a first reading you may ignore that material without loss of continuity. Later you may want to explore the notes.

———————

Let's start.

What is the neuroprocess hypothesis? The first part of this book supplies the answer. It begins with a chapter about our interaction with the world.

Part I

Neuroprocess
Hypothesis

2

Interaction with the World

This chapter and Chapter 3 lay the groundwork for the discussion of the neuroprocess hypothesis. Here we look at the way we interact with the world.

What is a *model*? There is no simple answer since the concept is used so widely. Here are some examples.

- *Models* who display dresses in a fashion show
- *Car models* of a particular design
- *Model species* that are mimicked by another species
- *Scale models* of airplanes in a wind tunnel
- *Weather models* forecasting the movement of hurricanes
- *Economic models* anticipating a recession

The last three are *models of the world*. In this chapter we examine the role of such models in our lives.

In the night sky some bright points of light seem to always move together, while others wander individually. Extensive research carried out over centuries eventually resulted in a mathematical model that not only classifies the two types of lights as stars and planets, but predicts their movement with reasonable precision. The astronomer and mathematician Johannes Kepler (1571–1630) accomplished this feat in 1627.[14] In particular, his model predicts that the planets move around the sun in elliptical orbits.

The results of the model are often cited as if they were facts of the world: The orbits of the planets around the sun are then claimed *to be* elliptical.

But that is not the case: The planets influence each other in ways that have proved to be mathematically intractable: While approximate formulas predict the movement for limited time intervals, we can only guess what will happen long-term.[15]

———————

The example isn't an unusual case of model interpretation. We generally conflate model output with facts of the world. We do this, for example, when models explain

- the bond forces within molecules
- the flow of electricity
- the strength of materials
- the conversion of heat into power in engines
- the vibrations of strings of a violin
- the echo in a valley
- the Great Depression

The conflation has provided us with deep insight into the world. Using that knowledge we have created equipment with miraculous performance: airplanes, computers, satellites, spacecraft, the global positioning system, artificial hearts, ... The list is endless.

Appropriately, the theoretical physicist and cosmologist Stephen Hawking called this conflation *model-dependent realism*.[16]

The conflation is aided by our experience that some of our sense perceptions—but by no means all—are shared by others.[17] Accordingly, these perceptions are in some sense impersonal, and we develop the feeling that they are facts of the world. That pragmatic view simplifies the interaction with others.

Stephen Hawking.[18]

But the conclusion that our perceptions are facts is unjustified. If a number of people agree with us on a sense perception, it only means that they have adopted similar or identical models.

Until recently, the construction of models didn't extend to the nervous system since suitable investigative tools didn't exist. That has changed. For example, functional magnetic resonance imaging (fMRI) allows us to observe the brain in action. These tools have produced a flood of diverse results.

The next chapter describes some of the new insights.

3
Results of Neuroscience

The human *nervous system* consists of the *brain*, the *spinal cord*, and the *network of nerves* that connect the brain and the spinal cord to other parts of the human body, for example, to the eyes, ears, organs, muscles, blood vessels, and glands.[19]

Neuroscientists have established a rich theory about the structure and performance of the nervous system. Here are some results about the brain.[20]

- The traditional view that each region of the brain is dedicated to particular functions has been replaced by the insight that neuroprocesses allocate regions dynamically, for example, for handling hearing, sight, smell, taste, and touch. Hence there is no visual brain, or auditory brain, or sense-of-touch brain.

- The neuroprocesses for the various functions compete with each other for space in the brain since there is only a finite amount of real estate, so to speak.

- Hours, days, weeks, and years after birth, neuroprocesses learn to interpret incoming signals and produce appropriate output. For example, they learn so that the person can grab items, interpret images, understand speech, walk, and talk.

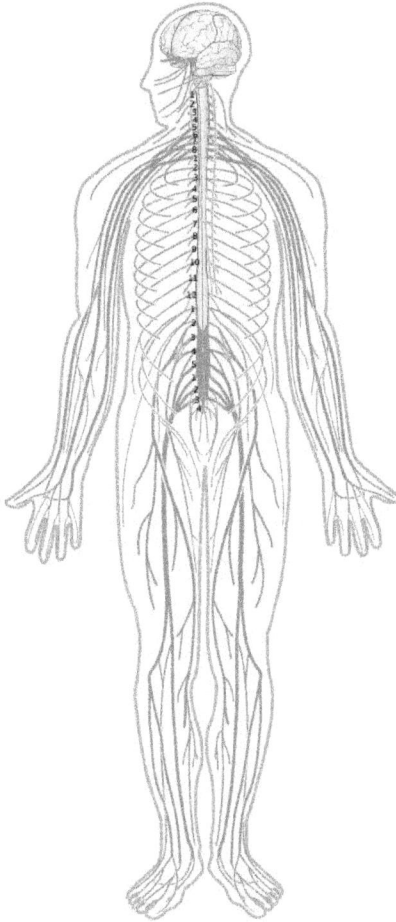

Nervous system diagram.[21]

Neuroprocesses can overcome the effects of catastrophic damage to the brain.[22]

- The neuroprocesses cope with misfortune—such as a person going blind, losing hearing, or losing a limb—by reallocating no-longer-needed capacity to existing functions.

- In exceptional cases, the neuroprocesses can reconfigure the brain even when half of the brain was removed at a very young age to combat an incurable disease.

A similar adjustment takes place when half of the brain is missing at birth.

- In cases of severe hearing loss, a cochlear implant captures sound and sends it electrically, through the cochlea, to the auditory nerve.[23] The neuroprocesses adapt to the new format of audio signals.

- For a deaf person, sound is sometimes converted externally to touch—that is, auditory signals become pressure signals on the skin. After a while, the person "hears" via the skin.

- For a blind person, images are sometimes converted to pressure on the skin. After some training, the person "sees" via the skin. When images are converted to electrotactile shocks on the tongue, the person eventually "sees" via the tongue. When images are converted to sound, a person begins to "see" via earbuds.

This may sound crazy, but is not. For the case of "seeing" with the tongue, brain imaging has shown that the signals received by the tongue are processed in an area of the brain that normally handles visual motion.

So far we have provided an intuitive understanding of neuroprocesses. The next chapter supplies details.

4

Fatigue

We are hiking in the mountains: We climb up slopes and descend into valleys, all the time enjoying the scenery. After four hours, we feel tired and decide to rest.[24]

Where does this feeling come from?

An obvious explanation is: The leg muscles determine that they have been stressed and are tired. They send corresponding information to the brain, which translates it to a feeling of fatigue.

Suppose that vague explanation is correct, and a person's statement such as "My legs are getting tired" captures the essence of the situation.

How then is the following possible?

In 1986, Georges Holtyzer of Belgium walked 418 miles in six and a half days. He was not permitted any stops for rest and moved almost 99 percent of the time.[25]

Why do we get a feeling of fatigue after four hours of hiking when Holtyzer could walk more than six days without rest?

Research into the causes of fatigue started in the 19th century. It led to the explanation that lack of oxygen and build-up of lactate caused muscle fatigue.

Exercise textbooks from the 1930s to today advance this theory.[26] Here are some problems with that claim:[27]

- Even at peak exertion, only about two-thirds of available muscle fibers are active.

- The feeling of fatigue is delayed when music is played during the activity—as is invariably done at exercise clubs around the world.

- When a wall clock is slowed down, people become tired later.

So, something else must be happening. The crucial insight came during the 2010s, when fatigue was recognized as an emotion:[28] The feeling of fatigue is produced by a subconscious neuroprocess to ensure that ongoing physical efforts don't overtax the body.

This insight supports the following explanation of fatigue:

- A subconscious neuroprocess analyzes the performance of the physical body and decides whether the current effort if continued not just for hours but days would cause damage. We aren't consciously aware of this analysis.

- Once the subconscious neuroprocess arrives at that conclusion, it outputs a feeling of fatigue. We recognize that feeling and decide to rest. We can restate this as: A conscious neuroprocess becomes aware of the feeling and concludes that rest is needed.

Thus, fatigue is an emotion that protects the body from harm.

The fatigue example is a special case of the following general situation.

- A subconscious neuroprocess receives input from outside or inside the body. Visual and audio signals are input examples from outside the body, while heart rate and oxygen saturation of the blood are input from the inside.

- The subconscious neuroprocess takes the input and produces various conclusions for conscious neuroprocesses. Example outputs are *feelings, images, interpreted audio,* and *interpreted writing.* The subconscious neuroprocess may also initiate *direct actions* that affect the body or the world.

The example list for the conclusions is woefully incomplete. In fact, we are unable to give a complete characterization of the possible cases. Instead, we simply declare all cases outside feelings and direct actions to be *unbidden thoughts.* The term "unbidden" reflects the fact that the thoughts pop up in consciousness and aren't the result of conscious reasoning.

For example, when a subconscious neuroprocess has analyzed a scene sensed by the eyes, we call the resulting image that pops into consciousness an unbidden thought.

As a result, from now we have just three types of output of subconscious neuroprocesses: feelings, unbidden thoughts, and direct actions. The feelings and unbidden thoughts are supplied to conscious neuroprocesses.

- *Feelings*: Examples are fatigue, fear, and joy.
- *Unbidden thoughts*: They suddenly pop up in consciousness. For example, a subconscious process initiates a panic attack by the frightening thought "My heart has stopped." Another case is the image resulting from visual information, or the recognition of spoken words from audio.
- *Direct actions*: Examples range from control of the heartbeat and respiratory rate to the movement of the fingers when a piano virtuoso plays a demanding concerto. In the latter case, the time available for triggering the movement of the fingers is far too short for conscious control.

The conscious neuroprocesses manipulate the feelings and unbidden thoughts supplied by the subconscious neuroprocesses using *deliberate thoughts,* and finally produce *decisions* and *actions.* We use the term "deliberate" for the thoughts since we can justify them by a logical argument or other explanation.

The direct actions of the subconscious neuroprocesses aren't part of the input for the conscious neuroprocesses. However, another subconscious neuroprocess may observe such an action and output its occurrence as an unbidden thought to consciousness. We say "may" since that step need not take place. For example, conscious neuroprocesses usually do not become aware of changes of the heart rate, while the knee jerk triggered by a tap below the knee is felt and seen.

You may wonder: The above definitions seemingly preclude that two subconscious neuroprocesses send information to each other. If we come upon two neuroprocesses with that feature, we eliminate the case conceptually by considering the two neuroprocesses to be just one neuroprocess. In some sense, we merge the two neuroprocesses.

We emphasize that the subconscious and conscious neuroprocesses are models of the actual processes in the human body. The discussion of Chapter 2 fully applies to these models. In particular, we invoke the idea of model-dependent realism and conflate model results with facts about the human body.

We may restate this as follows.

> *From now on, we act as if the subconscious and conscious neuroprocesses take place in the human body.*

Summary: The subconscious and conscious neuroprocesses described in this chapter are *models* of operations in the human body. For simplified discussions, we assume that the neuroprocesses *are* the actual operations.

We have defined the following inputs and outputs of the neuro-processes:

- Subconscious neuroprocess
  - input: information of body and world
  - output: feelings and unbidden thoughts for conscious neuro-processes, and direct actions
- Conscious neuroprocess
  - input: feelings and unbidden thoughts from subconscious neu-roprocesses
  - output: decisions and actions established via deliberate thoughts

---

The subconscious and conscious neuroprocesses so far look like static constructs that receive input and produce output. Actually, they interact in a complicated fashion, and even change as part of that activity. The next chapter has details.

5
Neuroprocess Hypothesis

According to the preceding chapter, an extremely conservative evaluation triggers the feeling of fatigue. It assumes that efforts will continue at the current level not just for hours, but for days.

Athletes competing in long-distance races eliminate that unjustified evaluation with proactive deliberate thoughts that modify the subconscious fatigue neuroprocess.

That change is not easy since the fatigue neuroprocess is not directly accessible: The runner can only engage in deliberate thoughts that gradually replace the fatigue neuroprocess by a different one supporting perseverance.

The famous Finnish distance runner Paavo Nurmi put it thus:[29]

> "Mind is everything. Muscles are pieces of rubber. All that I am, I am because of my mind."

The feelings of perseverance propel the runner until the body reaches its physical limit. This happens in one of two ways:[30]

- The runner has calibrated the effort so carefully that she is at the point of physical exhaustion just as she reaches the finish line. At that moment, perseverance is overtaken by fatigue, and the runner collapses. But minutes later, she is up again and celebrating.

- If the runner has miscalculated and exhaustion sets in before the end of the race, that calamity manifests itself in the "Full Foster" collapse position[31] where the runner crawls on elbows and knees and finally collapses before or after reaching the finish line. Regardless of the case, survival is threatened.

––––––––––

The modification of the subconscious fatigue neuroprocess by deliberate thoughts isn't an unusual interaction. Let's look at another example.

In traditional approaches to psychotherapy, the therapist helps the patient understand the problem. The patient then acts upon that insight.

Cognitive behavioral therapy (CBT) is different. It is based on the postulate that thought distortions result in destructive feelings and behavior. Hence, the therapist helps the patient to think differently, with the effect that the patient abandons the negative feelings and behavior.

The key statement is:

> *Our deliberate thoughts trigger our feelings, therefore changing our thoughts will change our feelings.*[32]

CBT has proved to be effective for a variety of disorders, for example, for depression, anxiety, alcohol and drug abuse, and eating disorders.[33]

Translated to the world of subconscious and conscious neuroprocesses, the main claim of CBT becomes:

> *Deliberate thoughts of conscious neuroprocesses influence subconscious neuroprocesses. In particular, the deliberate thoughts change feelings and unbidden thoughts produced by subconscious neuroprocesses.*

––––––––––

Two additional cases demonstrate the interaction of neuroprocesses. For purposeful walking, a subconscious neuroprocess determines the optimal speed so that the destination is reached with minimal total energy consumption.[34] The neuroprocess outputs feelings for different speeds. The optimal speed is associated with a feeling of comfortable achievement while other speeds produce feelings of impatience or discomfort. The neuroprocess determines the optimal speed within a few minutes of walking.[35]

We can readily change our walking speed from optimal to slower or faster values while ignoring the feeling of impatience or discomfort.

For example, we may want to arrive sooner due to some commitment, and thus walk at a brisk rate. Or we may decide to slow down to a crawl, for example when we visit an art gallery. In either case, the goal we are pursuing with the changed speed provides a pleasant feeling that overrides the negative emotion arising from the nonoptimal speed.

––––––––––––

When a piano virtuoso practices nine hours every day, she sharpens subconscious neuroprocesses that operate the fingers of her hands with lightning speed. During the concert, she doesn't consciously trigger each of these movements, but allows the neuroprocesses to operate the muscles. Instead, she focuses on the mood and tone and flow of the music. In some sense, she narrates the story of the composition.

She must update these subconscious neuroprocesses daily since otherwise the precision of muscle control deteriorates.

––––––––––––

Each of the above examples involves an extensive process connecting subconscious and conscious neuroprocesses.

In one direction, subconscious neuroprocesses produce feelings, trigger unbidden thoughts, and initiate direct actions. Except for some of the actions, we are aware of this information.

In the reverse direction, the actions, decisions, and deliberate thoughts of conscious neuroprocesses affect subconscious neuroprocesses. We see the effect indirectly through modified output of the subconscious neuroprocesses.

The exchange process isn't happening sporadically. Rather, it should be viewed as two rivers of information that continuously flow in both directions and change the neuroprocesses.

The neuroprocesses don't just evaluate input, carry out reasoning, and produce output. They also build and maintain information on a huge scale. In this book, the most important aspect is that they create and use a vast collection of *models of the world*. These models *are* the world as far as the neuroprocesses are concerned.

Before the advent of writing, the teaching of elders enhanced the learning of models for the conscious neuroprocesses. Once writing was available, some models were stored outside the body and could be acquired by reading.

We view the models of the world to be part of the neuroprocesses in the same sense that a computer program may reuse internal data it built previously.

The following hypothesis—the *neuroprocess hypothesis*—summarizes the two key features of the neuroprocesses established in this chapter.

> *The neuroprocesses change continuously. In particular, they modify each other.*

> *The neuroprocesses consider the* models *of the world that they create to be* facts *of the world.*

Summary: The neuroprocess hypothesis says that subconscious and conscious neuroprocesses build models of the world and influence each other in a dynamic process.

The models of the world are facts of the world as far as the neuro-processes are concerned.

The next chapter shows that the neuroprocess hypothesis is consistent with the results of neuroscience.

6

Justification

Chapters 3–5 cite a number of results that directly or indirectly support the concept of subconscious and conscious neuroprocesses and the neuroprocess hypothesis.

Complete validation demands more: We must show that the concept is consistent with relevant results of neuroscience. It is a Herculean task since neuroscience has produced an ocean of results at both low and high levels of detail.

- Results at low level cover the behavior of *cells* and other elementary building blocks. Here are examples. *Grid cells* of periodic triangular or hexagonal arrays are part of the brain's metric for the representation of space. *Place cells* represent specific positions in space. *Head-direction cells* define the direction in which the head is pointed.[36]

- Results at high level concern *features* of the nervous system and their interaction. Example results link the perception of *events* and *memory*.[37]

Three books summarize the parts of the theory connected with the neuroprocess hypothesis in exemplary fashion.

- *Livewired* by David Eagleman[38] lays out the miraculous performance of the brain and, more generally, the nervous system.

- *Physical Intelligence* by Scott Grafton[39] vividly describes the intricate web of connections linking, in the words of the book, "body and mind."

- *Emotional* by Leonard Mlodinow[40] lays out key results of *affective neuroscience*, which investigates the fascinating connection of subconsciously produced emotions and consciously made decisions.

The definition of the subconscious and conscious neuroprocesses and the neuroprocess hypothesis is consistent not only with the results described in these books, but also with the following material.

- *Feeling & Knowing* by Antonio Damasio[41] explains that the drive for survival produced the nervous system. One may rewrite the steps and obtain a story about the development of the neuroprocesses.

- *Breath* by James Nestor[42] tells how breathing influences our well-being. The story can be recast using neuroprocesses.[43]

- *Thinking, Fast and Slow* by Daniel Kahneman[44] analyzes fast and slow thinking. Fast thinking can be viewed as part of unbidden thought output of subconscious neuroprocesses, while slow thinking is connected with deliberate thoughts of conscious neuroprocesses.

- *Full Catastrophe Living* by Jon Kabat-Zinn[45] proposes *mindfulness* as a key tool for managing our lives. The meditation achieving mindfulness essentially is training of subconscious neuroprocesses by conscious thoughts.[46]

- The introduction to the National Academy of Sciences colloquium "Brain Produces Mind by Modeling" in 2019 includes the following statement:[47]

    "An intriguing possibility is that the brain produces the mind by forming a model of the entire environment including the body, the physical environment, other agents, and the social environment. It uses this model to learn, decide, attend, remember, perceive and produce action."

The intriguing possibility becomes a version of the neuroprocess hypothesis when we expand its single model to interacting subconscious and conscious neuroprocesses.

- In an entirely different approach, mathematical arguments mandate the existence of models in the brain.

   "The living brain, so far as it is to be successful and efficient as a regulator for survival, *must* proceed, in learning, by the formation of a model (or models) of its environment."[48]

The reference doesn't assert any details about the models, for example, how they fit together or influence each other. But it supports the claim that the neuroprocesses build and use models of the world.

———————

Summary: There is ample evidence justifying the concept of subconscious and conscious neuroprocesses and the related neuroprocess hypothesis.

———————

The next chapter summarizes the material about neuroprocesses. You may find it useful later when you read Parts II and III.

7

Summary

Here are the key results of Chapters 1–6.

Terminology:[49]

- *Subconscious* and *conscious neuroprocesses* represent the activities of the human body that involve information acquisition, evaluation, and control in any form.
- *Mind* is the awareness of the conscious neuroprocesses as they take place.
- *Intelligence* is demonstrated by the neuroprocesses when they achieve their goals.
- *Neuroscience* includes all aspects of neuroprocesses.

Input and output of neuroprocesses:[50]

- Subconscious neuroprocesses
  - input: information of body and world
  - output: feelings and unbidden thoughts for conscious neuroprocesses, and direct actions
- Conscious neuroprocesses
  - input: feelings and unbidden thoughts from subconscious neuroprocesses
  - output: decisions and actions established via deliberate thoughts

Neuroprocess hypothesis:[51]

> *The neuroprocesses change continuously. In particular, they modify each other.*

> *The neuroprocesses consider the* models *of the world that they create and use to be* facts *of the world.*

We are ready to analyze philosophical claims, problems, and questions.

The chapters of the next part analyze fallacies caused by the erroneous viewpoint that reasoning is carried out by an input/output machine, or at least is performed with the precision of such a machine.

Part II

Fallacies

8

The Platonic World

Where does the concept of time come from, or the thought that the sequence of numbers 1, 2, 3, . . . continues forever, or the idea of a geometry of lines and points, or the perception that roses are beautiful? We don't find any of these ideas in nature. So how is it possible that we can think of them?

Plato. Luni marble.[52]

The philosopher Plato (c. 424–c. 348 BCE) offered a comprehensive answer to these and related questions. With some modification, his explanation is widely accepted even today.

He claimed that there is a *world of ideas* beyond the natural world. The postulated world contains timeless, absolute, and unchangeable ideas that we do not sense and can only think about.[53] Examples are the concepts of time, number, beauty, and quality.[54]

The world of ideas is also called the *world of essences* or the *Platonic world*. The *theory of forms*[55] describes the rules governing that world.

Why would Plato come up with the world of ideas? And why has it survived for 2,400 years?

Our answer: Plato and many philosophers of subsequent centuries perceived that all thinking and reasoning was done as if by an input/output machine.

For Plato, there actually was such a machine: the heart.[56] Once Galen (129–c. 210) claimed that the brain was the source of emotions and thoughts,[57] the brain replaced the heart. As late as 1968, the computer HAL in the movie "2001: A Space Odyssey" supposedly reasoned like humans,[58] but actually was just an input/output machine.

Plato and subsequent philosophers correctly considered the processes of an input/output machine to be too limited to create timeless, absolute, and unchangeable concepts.

For example, when an ancient mathematician drew straight lines in the sand, he viewed them as an imperfect representation of idealized lines that were perfectly straight and had no width. Two intersecting lines met at an idealized point. Where did these idealized lines and points come from? An input/output machine seemingly couldn't produce that abstraction. Plato explained the existence of idealized lines and points by declaring them to be part of a world of ideas.

That world contained all abstract concepts—for example, beauty, time, and quality—that an input/output machine couldn't create.

In contrast, the neuroprocess hypothesis postulates that subconscious and conscious neuroprocesses carry out sophisticated reasoning and even change each other. Chapter 3 cites a number of examples demonstrating the extraordinary performance of neuroprocesses.

Here are additional examples, taken in part from Chapters 4–6.

- Neuroprocesses establish the need for rest during hikes under the assumption that the effort will continue not just for hours but for days. The neuroprocesses assemble and evaluate the relevant information and act upon it.[59]

- Neuroprocesses compute optimal walking speed within minutes of hiking. At the conscious level, the decision corresponds to a feeling of comfortable achievement.

  We see how extraordinary this feat is when we compare the task with the much simpler problem of optimizing the glide speed of an airplane. The latter problem requires a complicated mathematical formulation and can only be solved with sophisticated optimization methods. Due to the complexity of the methods, a simple approximation is used in practice.[60]

- A piano virtuoso executes 29,656 individual notes when performing the Rachmaninoff Piano Concerto #3. She must play each note with particular emphasis and rhythm to create a narrative. And all this from memory.[61] In the terminology of neuroprocesses, the pianist's practice of the concerto is a training program where subconscious neuroprocesses learn how to operate the fingers at lightning speed. During the performance, she relies on these neuroprocesses as well as conscious ones.

- Neuroprocesses handle subtle differences of cases with high precision.[62] For example, when subconscious and conscious neuroprocesses interpret visual information of lines in the sand, the output depends on the situation. An artist viewing the sand's landscape might see the lines as an interesting shape change. For an engineer the lines may be channels that could guide the flow of water. A mathematician may see them as abstract lines of zero width.

- Neuroprocesses manipulate language and memory with mind-boggling dexterity. A theory explains aspects of this performance by postulating *conceptual spaces*. The spaces are geometric structures whose dimensions represent qualities such as weight, color, and temperature. Properties correspond to subspaces.[63]

- Empirical esthetics—the scientific approach to the study of aesthetic perceptions of art, music, or any object that can give rise to aesthetic judgments—now has the sub-discipline of *neuroesthetics*.[64] Researchers in that area study the neuroprocesses when a person contemplates or creates works of art. It is a first attempt to connect concepts such as quality and beauty with neuroprocesses.

- Neuroprocesses rely on physical representation involving grid cells, place cells, and head-direction cells in the brain to navigate in space. Effectively, the neuroprocesses create a physical Euclidean geometry with cells.[65]

This is just a small sampling of the vast number of results obtained in a few decades of research.[66] Imagine how much more we will find out about neuroprocesses in the not so distant future! Most likely we will discover that they are miracle performers.

We may be tempted to claim that the results to-date and our projection for the future *prove* that the world of ideas does not exist. But that would be wrong. Isn't it possible that the neuroprocesses look at the world of ideas while they perform miraculous feats?

How can we then establish that the world of ideas doesn't exist? Is this even possible? If not, can we establish a weaker conclusion, for example, that the world of ideas is not needed?

We need an important concept of science for the answers. Suppose two theories explain a phenomenon equally well. Which theory should we accept?

Somebody might say, "Why not keep both of them? It certainly would do no harm." Actually, it would. If scientists accepted all theories that explain an effect with equal accuracy, there would be an enormous redundancy of theories. The flood of results would slow down and eventually prevent verification of new theories, thus stopping scientific progress.

Hence we should give up one of the two theories. The universally accepted rule for that decision is *Occam's razor*.[67] The original version says that, if two theories explain some phenomenon equally well, the simpler one should be accepted and the more complicated one rejected. Only 700 years old, the rule is a formalization of the pragmatic idea that we should avoid confusion created by redundant concepts. Viewed that way, Occam's razor is one of the principles of evolution.

Subsequent versions of Occam's razor depend on different interpretation of "simpler." For example, Bertrand Russell (1872–1970) proposes the following principle.[68]

> "Whenever possible, substitute constructions out of known entities for inferences to unknown entities."

We use a variation of Russell's interpretation that relies on presence and absence of validation as the criterion.

> Suppose two theories explain some situation equally well. We prefer one of them over the other if the following holds.
>
> • The accepted theory has been partially or fully validated.
> • The rejected theory hasn't been, and likely never will be, validated.

Though the rule is based on a particular interpretation of "simpler," we will not invent a new term for it and simply call it *Occam's razor* from now on. We differentiate this from the original statement by calling the latter the *original version of Occam's razor*.

Here is an example. The aether of physics supposedly was required for the propagation of electromagnetic and gravitational forces.[69]

The Michelson-Morley experiment of 1887 and subsequent more precise tests ruled out the existence of the aether up to a certain level of accuracy.[70]

No such test can ever *prove* that there is no aether, since an even more subtle test might deliver the opposite conclusion. But that outcome seems so unlikely that present-day physicists don't pursue such a proof. On the other hand, today's validated models of the physical world make no use of the aether concept. Occam's razor then sounds the death knell for the aether.

_____

Let's return to the discussion about the world of ideas. We only need the experimentally justified concept of subconscious and conscious neuroprocesses and their complex interaction to explain how we come up with novel ideas and concepts.

For example, the existence of grid cells, place cells, and head-direction cells proves that neuroprocesses create a physical Euclidean geometry in the brain. We surely wouldn't attribute this result of evolution to the existence of a world of ideas.

On the other hand, the world of ideas has not been, and never will be, validated. That conclusion follows directly from the definition of the world of ideas: It claims that we cannot sense it and only think about it.

Then Occam's razor advises us to abandon the world of ideas.

We emphasize that the conclusion does not *prove* that the world of ideas doesn't exist. It shows that we don't *need* that world to explain how we develop ideas and concepts. The scientifically proven features of the neuroprocesses supply the proof.

These considerations have an important corollary. Any person who objects to the use of Occam's razor will not accept the above arguments and may insist that there is a world of ideas.

Part IV explains that this reaction is an instance where certain neuroprocesses prevent resolution of philosophical problems. For any such case, there is only one reasonable reaction: We stop participating in the discussion.

Summary: Two arguments establish that the world of ideas is not needed.

- The neuroprocess hypothesis suffices to establish that the neuroprocesses have an extraordinary capacity for creating and manipulating ideas and concepts. Experimental results confirm this conclusion.
- The world of ideas cannot be confirmed by any test by its very definition. Occam's razor then banishes the world of ideas as unnecessary.

Can you see that we have come to a watershed in philosophy? Until recently, some claims of that field may have seemed odd but couldn't be refuted due to the very nature of the postulates. At the same time, a proof of validity either wasn't possible or wasn't supplied and couldn't be expected in the future.

Neuroscience has begun to offer different explanations that are supported by experiments. This may produce an upheaval in philosophy. We say "may" since rejection of tools of science such as Occam's razor will render the explanations useless.

The next chapter investigates two philosophical claims about mathematics with Occam's razor as the main tool.

9

Natural, Discovered Mathematics

Where do the numbers, the basic building blocks of mathematics, come from? They seemingly are part of nature since counting things is an integral part of our lives. But we cannot point to anything in nature that we could call number.

The same arguments apply to all of mathematics: Is it part of nature and we discover it, or do we invent it?

Let's rephrase the question in the form of two claims that we would like to settle.

- Mathematics is part of nature.

- Mathematics is discovered and not invented.

The two statements are part of a minefield of philosophical arguments about the origin and substance of mathematics.[71]

An irrational part of the discussion is evident from the leading paragraph of Wikipedia's "Leonhard Euler" entry:

> "... [Euler] *founded* the studies of graph theory and topology and *made* pioneering and influential *discoveries* in many other branches of mathematics ... He *introduced* much of modern mathematical terminology and notation ... " [emphasis added]

How could Euler *found* and *introduce* and simultaneously *make discoveries*, when each of these steps obviously involved the same neuroprocesses?

In this chapter, we show with simple arguments that the two claims about mathematics are superfluous and should be discarded.

We begin with the declaration that mathematics is part of nature. There are arguments for and against.[72] Three papers deserve special mention. Two of them[73] cite instances where mathematical models predict detailed results of the physical sciences and engineering. These results seemingly support the claim that mathematics is somehow part of nature. The third paper[74] argues that these instances are cherry-picked and that a multitude of erroneous mathematical predictions is ignored.[75]

We don't add here to those arguments. Rather, we show that the neuroprocess hypothesis makes the postulated existence of mathematics in nature superfluous. The discussion also clarifies why mathematical predictions about nature often turn out to be correct.

Here is a simple argument that seemingly proves mathematics to be part of nature. When we move one apple next to another one, we have two apples side by side. When we add one more, we have three apples. This happens no matter when and where we do this.

Just by that argument, we seemingly have established the foundation for mathematics in nature. Indeed, the thought of the apples has a mesmerizing effect. With the picture of the three apples in mind, we cannot shake the thought that mathematics is part of nature, independent of our existence.

Convincing as the picture seems to be, there is a different explanation for the origin of mathematics.

We have a pile of apples. We remove one apple at a time and set it aside. Later we reverse the process and put the apples back, one at a time. We are convinced that a pile of same size results.

Why are we so sure? We certainly don't *know* this. Instead, we build subconscious neuroprocesses as a baby and toddler that we can move things back and forth without any loss. The game of peekaboo helps create these neuroprocesses, as do experiences using blocks.

The neuroprocesses often need refinement. When a toddler inadvertently lets go of a balloon, she is stunned and upset. The crying is as much a reaction to the loss as to the surprise: The prediction that things don't go away when one lets go of them, needs correction. Other surprises are a snowball melting on a stove and a large amount of bath tub water disappearing quickly down a drain.

We see that the permanence of apples is not a natural event that we *know* of and can rely on for the foundation of mathematics, but rather is a conclusion of subconscious and conscious neuroprocesses.

As we engage in the above thoughts, the earlier argument that one, two, and three apples prove mathematics to be part of nature loses its hypnotic effect. After all, neuroprocesses assure us that combining and separating apples doesn't cause losses or gains.

As for the numbers 1, 2, and 3: They have a complex history where originally there were pebbles, marks in sand, or scratches in clay tablets that corresponded to apples. Conscious neuroprocesses arrived at that correspondence and eventually produced[76] the simplifying symbols "1," "2," and "3."

We can go on and reformulate the development of all of mathematics as construction by conscious neuroprocesses. Much of that development has been worked out in texts on the history of mathematics.[77]

The conclusion that conscious neuroprocesses produced mathematics while looking at the world clarifies why mathematics sometimes make precise predictions: After all, the forecasts are not about the *behavior* of the natural world, but about the *output of models* of the natural world created by neuroprocesses.

Many times the models of the world are too complex for mathematics to handle. One might argue that this may be true for current mathematics and that we will resolve this in the future.

That forecast is not correct. There are models of the world where mathematics has *proved* that we will never be able to make mathematical predictions. For example, we will never be able determine the long-term configuration of our solar system. The best we can do is simulation of the configuration over a limited time horizon.[78]

We see here that the existence of subconscious and conscious neuroprocesses readily explains the ingenuity inherent in mathematics—the uncanny match with natural events, the permanence of results, and the extraordinary complexity of this most beautiful construction of mankind.

On the other hand, experimental verification cannot possibly prove that mathematics is part of nature. Where would one find the numbers, the symbols, the theorems?

Accordingly, we apply Occam's razor and reject that mathematics is part of nature.

There is another good, pragmatic, reason for that conclusion. The history of mathematics is replete with cases where arguments based on nature misled mathematicians and resulted in wrong theorems or wrong proofs for correct theorems. An example for the second case is the erroneous validation of calculus by Isaac Newton (1643–1727).[79]

Another, very different argument casts doubt on the claim that mathematics is part of nature: Some mathematical theorems are in direct conflict with well-accepted results about nature. Here is an example.

We have several baskets, each containing some items. It's easy to do the following: We reach into each basket and extract one item. If we have enough helpers, we can do the extraction step simultaneously for all baskets.

Consider the more complicated case where we want to carry out the simultaneous extraction for an infinite number of baskets. It's difficult to imagine how this could be accomplished. The *axiom of choice*[80] nevertheless postulates that this can be done.

Invoking that axiom, Stefan Banach (1892–1945) and Alfred Tarski (1901–1983) derived in 1924 the following result about the world, now known as the *Banach-Tarski paradox*.

Using the axiom of choice, one may divide a solid 3-dimensional sphere into a great many small pieces in such a way that these very pieces can be reassembled to become *two* solid 3-dimensional spheres with the *same* diameter as the original one.[81]

In short, the axiom of choice allows a doubling of material. Needless to say, this violates basic models of the world.

Did that result cause mathematicians to shun the axiom of choice? For a while, heated arguments for and against the axiom created a poisonous atmosphere.[82] Today most mathematicians consider the axiom of choice an important part of mathematics. If you ask why, they explain that the axiom allows proofs of impressive theorems.[83]

———

Let's turn to the second claim that mathematics is discovered. There has never been—and there never will be—scientific verification, for the simple reason that the claim postulates an ephemeral prior existence. Nevertheless, the following arguments seemingly are ironclad proof that mathematics is discovered.

Once we have proved a mathematical result, it isn't just valid, but will be valid forever. More importantly, the result must have been valid in the past since the logic-based proof doesn't depend on timing. This means that all mathematical results that have been or can ever be proved, exist not only now but must have existed already in the past. Hence, these results can only be discovered.[84]

This argument doesn't affect the conclusion that the discovery claim involves an ephemeral prior world whose existence cannot possibly be proved: The fact that we can imagine something doesn't mean that the something actually exists. On the other hand, the science-based neuroprocess hypothesis explains how mathematics comes about. Given these two considerations, Occam's razor advises us to drop the discovery claim.

Practical aspects of the construction of mathematics lend intuitively appealing support to this conclusion, as we see next.

Does the thought "The results we are proving today existed in the past" help mathematicians achieve more than if they just say "The neuroprocesses produce mathematical results"?

We would say, "No." The task of proving a mathematical claim doesn't become any easier if one believes the result exists already somewhere, instead of thinking, "We should be able to prove this."

There is a psychological aspect of the discovery claim. Sometimes a mathematician may say, "I *know* that this is correct," whatever "this" is. At that moment, there is a mental image that the result resides somewhere. This might seem helpful, but becomes detrimental when it is the only way to think about possible results. In contrast, the mathematician seeing herself as an inventor and not as a discoverer is not prejudiced by that thought and may dream up seemingly wacky but extraordinary results.

In recent decades this has been happening in computational mathematics. Unusual thinking has produced stunning results.

For example, there is a quite simple algorithm[85] that in 19 iterations computes the first 100 billion ($= 100,000,000,000$) digits of $1/\pi$, where $\pi = 3.1415\ldots$

Another unusual algorithm computes the nth digit of π directly for any value of n, without computing the first $n - 1$ digits.[86]

Way-out ideas such as these[87] weren't fostered by thoughts of mathematical discovery, but by a spirit of unfettered invention.

Here is a related quote by the mathematician Jonathan Borwein:[88]

> "Mathematics is a human endeavor. It takes part in and adapts itself to culture. It is not a question of abstract reality, immutable, eternal, unearthly constructs as conceived of by Frege.
>
> "Mathematical knowledge is not infallible. In concert with empirical science, mathematics can move forward while errors are made, then corrected, and then perhaps corrected again. This flawed nature of the subject is brilliantly described in *Proofs and Refutations* by Lakatos.[89]

Jonathan Borwein.[90]

> "There exist several conceptions of proof and of mathematical rigor, as a function of time, place and other considerations. The use of computers to construct proofs constitutes a nontraditional version of rigor.

"Empirical evidence, numerical techniques, and probabilistic evidence help all of us to decide what ought to be believed as true in mathematics. Aristotelean logic isn't always the best means to come to a decision."

While Borwein envisions a future mathematics that redefines rigor, Stephen Wolfram—computer scientist, physicist, and chief designer of the famous *Mathematica* and *Wolfram Alpha* software—lays out a revolutionary construction of all of mathematics.[91]

Stephen Wolfram.[92]

It relies on elementary computations and classifies the axioms of current mathematics as just one of a fantastically large number of possible outcomes. In one demonstration he creates a variety of logic axioms. The propositional logic of present-day mathematics is created by an axiom near case number 50,000 of the construction process.

In a much more elaborate development, he shows that all constructions of mathematics can be traced back to a structure called the *ruliad*.[93] .

There is an important aspect of Wolfram's construction that is not covered by his method. Imagine each system of axioms to be a drop of water in a vast ocean of cases.

How is one to decide which drops are interesting? The answer: We need to work out evaluation methods, a difficult task. In this context, the discovery claim is irrelevant for the systematic construction of mathematics and useless for the evaluation.

———————————

Summary: The postulate that mathematics is part of nature is an unprovable claim. The same applies to the discovery postulate since it claims an ephemeral existence. On the other hand, the neuroprocess hypothesis produces science-based explanations for the development of mathematics. Hence Occam's razor advises that we abandon both postulates.

Conclusions about the construction, evaluation, and use of mathematics further demonstrate the irrelevance of both postulates.

———————————

Overarching principles that go far beyond day-to-day practical rules are core achievements of philosophy. On the surface, the results seem justified. But the supposed universality of the principles is their Achilles heel: Detailed examination may reveal that they put up unattainable goals. We see an example in the next chapter.

10

Consistency

How should we develop a scientific theory about a complex situation? A too-broad search for theory candidates will dissipate our effort and won't produce any tangible results, while a too-narrow focus based on current knowledge won't result in anything interesting. So how should we proceed?

Karl Popper.[94]

Karl Raimund Popper (1902–1994), one of the 20th century's most influential philosophers of science, addressed this question and recommended four steps for the development of scientific theories.[95]

1. Test the proposed theory for internal consistency by comparing its various conclusions.

2. Investigate the logical form of the theory, with the goal of determining whether it is indeed an empirical or scientific theory and not something else, like a tautology.

3. Compare the theory with other theories, mainly to determine whether it constitutes a scientific advance.

4. Test the validity of the theory through empirical application of its conclusions.

On the surface, these steps look appealing. However, closer examination reveals fundamental problems. We examine the first step here and the remainder in Chapter 15.

The test of internal consistency demanded in the first step seems essential since an inconsistency empowers the theory to prove *any* claim, as follows.

Suppose that statements A, B, and C define a theory and are inconsistent. That is, they cannot simultaneously be true. Then for *any* statement S, the claim "A, B, and C imply S" is correct and thus S is a conclusion of the theory.[96]

So the attractiveness of the first step is not in question. But can the first step always be done?

The answer is an emphatic "No."

Today we still don't know whether some theories that have been used for centuries are internally consistent! We also don't know the extent to which neuroprocesses are inconsistent. Let's look at example cases.

In 1931, Kurt Gödel (1906–1978) proved the following result, today called his *second incompleteness theorem*: For any consistent system of axioms that contains a certain amount of elementary arithmetic, consistency of the system cannot be proved in that system.[97]

The axioms specified in Gödel's theorem are part of a huge number of theories of the natural sciences. Hence, consistency of these theories is in doubt and in the most general case cannot be proved.

In physics, important theories clash. Examples are the theory of relativity and quantum physics. The theory of relativity is invoked to correct the clocks in the satellites of the Global Positioning System. The results of quantum physics are essential for the design of computer chips.

The two theories collide in profound ways. *Schrödinger's cat* and *quantum entanglement* demonstrate the conflict. In the first case, a cat in a box is alive or dead depending on a random subatomic event that may or may not occur.[98] In the second case, the quantum state of each particle of a group cannot be described independently of the state of the others, no matter how far the particles are dispersed.[99]

Since subconscious and conscious neuroprocesses change continuously, there is no way to assure consistency.

At best, we can try to analyze inconsistencies as they show up and correct them through deliberate thoughts if possible. We say "if possible" since sometimes the neuroprocesses can't be changed.

Here are two situations that involve subconscious neuroprocesses. The description is taken from our earlier book on models.[100]

We are shown the picture below and are asked about the color of the two squares labeled "A" in the topmost row and "B" next to the cylinder. More specifically, how do the pixels of squares A and B differ?

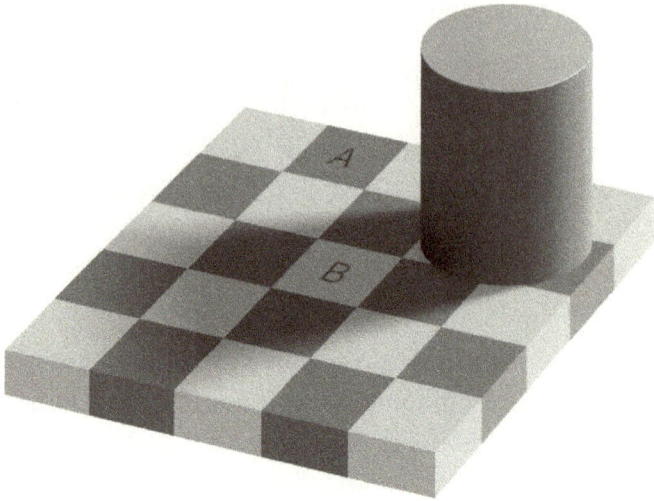

Perception: Square A is much darker than square B.[101]

The answer is obvious: The pixels of A are black and those of B are white. If we want to be more precise and avoid the extreme terms "black" and "white," we may instead declare that the pixels of A are much darker than those of B.

Next we are shown a quite similar picture.

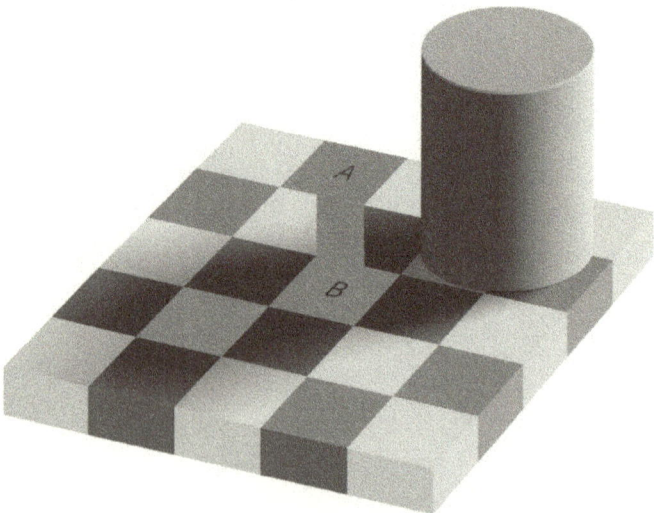

Reality: Squares A and B are the same shade of gray.[102]

The only change is that the squares A and B have been connected by a corridor that has exactly the same gray shade as both A and B. We suddenly realize that our answer was wrong.

Incredulous, we go back to the first picture. Once more we become certain that A and B are differently colored. Moving to the second picture, we see again that this conclusion is wrong. In fact, we can go back and forth as often as we like and each time experience this effect.

What is happening here?

In the first picture, a subconscious neuroprocess determines color while taking the shading effect of the column into account.

In the evaluation of the second picture, a subconscious neuroprocess relies on the rule that a contiguous area that looks uniformly colored is indeed uniformly colored. That neuroprocess is used to evaluate the area composed of A, B, and the connecting corridor.

The next situation involves geometric shape instead of color. How do the two parallelograms in the drawing below differ?

Two parallelograms as table surfaces.[103]

The answer is obvious: The left parallelogram is much longer and slimmer than the right one.

Now strip away the legs and moldings of the tables.

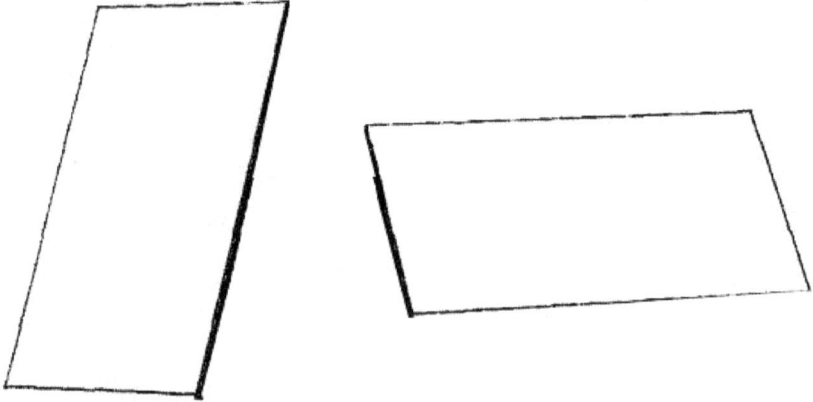

The two parallelograms seen by themselves.[104]

The right parallelogram is now seen as a rotated version of the left one.[105] We confirm this by measuring with a ruler.

Given that knowledge, we go back to the first picture: The two parallelograms become different again.

In both situations, we cannot change the subconscious neuroprocesses with deliberate thoughts, not matter how hard we try. We call such neuroprocesses *immutable*.

———————

Evidently, demanding a consistency check of every proposed theory prior to its use is a utopian demand. Instead, we should use a pragmatic construction method just as employed by the neuroprocesses where we don't test for consistency after each constructive step, but attempt to resolve inconsistencies as they surface. This isn't always possible, as we have seen.

A similar attitude has also prevailed in mathematics. For example, when Carl Friedrich Gauss (1777–1855), Nikolai Lobachevsky (1792–1856), and János Bolyai (1802–1860) independently developed hyperbolic geometry in the first part of the 19th century, it wasn't clear if it was consistent.[106]

Decades later, Eugenio Beltrami (1835–1900) proved that Euclidean and hyperbolic geometry were either both consistent or both inconsistent.[107]

In the 20th century, Alfred Tarski (1901–1983) defined axioms for a substantial fragment of Euclidean geometry and proved consistency.[108] That was 2300 years after Euclid (mid 4th–mid 3rd century BCE) defined that geometry.

Summary: Demanding a consistency check for scientific theories is a utopian demand. Instead, we should adopt a pragmatic attitude where we fix inconsistencies as they surface.

Sometimes a repair is not possible and we must accept inconsistencies. We then use the theories in restricted settings. The clashing theories of relativity and quantum physics are examples, as is the restricted use of Newton's universe.

In the 20th century, the work of the philosopher Ludwig Wittgenstein (1889–1951) had a huge impact on philosophy. We employ the neuroprocess hypothesis in the next chapter to analyze his famous book *Tractatus Logico-Philosophicus*.

11

Tractatus Logico-Philosophicus

Somebody claims, "The moon is east of voltage." What an odd thing to say! Though the sentence complies with the rules of grammar, the way it combines the planet, a direction, and a concept of electricity doesn't make sense. So we declare the statement to be *nonsensical*.

Is it always that easy to unmask nonsensical statements? The answer is: No, it can be quite difficult. We see examples in later chapters. This raises the following question: Is there a reliable, possibly time-consuming, method to identify nonsensical statements?

The philosopher Ludwig Wittgenstein (1889–1951) created two landmark books that address the latter question: the *Tractatus Logico-Philosophicus*,[109] *Tractatus* for short, and the *Philosophical Investigations*.[110]

The *Tractatus* is an amazing attempt to establish what can and cannot be expressed by language. The *Philosophical Investigations* supplies a powerful method for the analysis of philosophical statements and questions.

In our opinion, the depth and profundity of these works and the books compiled later from Wittgenstein's notes establish him as the greatest philosopher of the 20th century.

Ludwig Wittgenstein.[111]

Wittgenstein published the *Tractatus* in 1921. In the second half of the 1920s, Wittgenstein realized that the *Tractatus* contained "grave mistakes" (German *schwere Irrtümer*) that could not be remedied.[112]

Essentially, the *Tractatus* tried to eliminate inappropriate—for example, metaphysical—language, but also excluded legitimate communication.

Below we use the neuroprocess hypothesis to identify the error.

First, we need an intuitive understanding of the main ideas of the *Tractatus*: *logical atomism* and the *picture theory*.

————————

Logical atomism postulates that each thing of the world can be described by some logic formula that references smaller things. Each smaller thing can be described by another logic formula that uses even smaller things. Each of these logic formulas is a *fact*.

The process eventually stops with *elementary things* that cannot be described in terms of yet smaller things. They have names but no properties. Indeed, if they did have properties, they could be defined via even smaller things.

The logical formulas that reference only elementary things are *elementary facts.*

When we reverse the process, we construct from elementary facts all facts that could ever occur in the world.

The *picture theory* relies on logical atomism. It postulates that thoughts, and hence language, reflect the logical relationships of things—the facts—in the same sense that the technical drawing of a radio depicts with lines and certain symbols how the wires connect the components of the radio. In some sense, all language statements are logically correct *pictures* of the world.

This conclusion imposes a severe limitation on what language can ever express. While language can formulate a vast number of statements about facts and things that are part of the world, it cannot step beyond and talk about anything *outside* the world.

This conclusion creates a fundamental problem: The *Tractatus* contains a large number of statements about things beyond the world— for example, the description of the picture theory—yet claims that such statements are not possible.

Wittgenstein attempts to resolve this inconsistency with a famous ladder statement where he compares reading the *Tractatus* with climbing a ladder. The reader throws the ladder away upon achieving the desired insight.[113]

Let's evaluate the claims of the *Tractatus* using the neuroprocess hypothesis of Chapter 5. The hypothesis states that the subconscious and conscious neuroprocesses have only models of the world available and not facts. This implies that the models may differ from person to person. In fact, they often do, as discussions reveal.

This proves that human communication doesn't use the things and facts of logical atomism as stated in the picture theory. Accordingly, the core claims of the *Tractatus* are not valid.

Since the models of the world may differ from person to person, how do we know that any person can understand us?

The answer: We *don't* know this. When we tell a person something, we also operate neuroprocesses that anticipate the reaction of the person.[114]

If the reaction agrees with the anticipated response, we assume that the person has understood the statement.

If there is a different reaction, we clarify the statement. The exchange process stops when the person's reaction agrees with our anticipation.

If we cannot reach that stage in a few trials, we simply give up. Examples of frustrated final statements are "I don't think we can work together," "This isn't going to work out," or "Let's agree to disagree."

Summary: The neuroprocess hypothesis shows that the core concepts of the *Tractatus*—logical atomism and the picture theory—are untenable. This conclusion destroys the foundation of the *Tractatus*.

After the failure of the *Tractatus*, Wittgenstein developed a powerful method that could be applied to virtually every philosophical problem. He called it *language games*.

We use his method in the next chapter as we investigate a philosophical problem that has been debated for more than 2,000 years.

The chapter starts Part III of the book, titled *Clarity*. We use that bold term since Wittgenstein's method of language games is a powerful tool for achieving clarity about difficult philosophical questions.

Part III

Clarity

12

Knowledge = Justified True Belief

We know that $1 + 1 = 2$, that the moon is smaller than the earth, and that a week consists of seven days. In each case, we can explain why we know this.

Do we have knowledge for which we have no explanation? More broadly, what is knowledge? The latter question is one of the major open problems of philosophy.[115]

Plato (c. 424–c. 348 BCE) postulated that knowledge is *justified true belief*. That concept is defined as follows. We *know* something to be true if that something is *true*, we *believe* that, and can *justify* that belief.

There are arguments for and against Plato's definition.[116] Using the neuroprocess hypothesis, we will see that it is flawed.

We begin with a short dialogue.

> Mary: "I *know* that this doesn't work."
> Peter: "How can you be so sure?"
> Mary: "I just have a feeling about this."
> Peter: "That's not a good reason."
> Mary: "For me it is."
> After a while:
> Mary: "See, I *knew* it wouldn't work."

What is happening? Information about the situation flows into some of Mary's subconscious neuroprocesses and is evaluated. A feeling emerges that this—whatever "this" is in the discussion—won't work.

Mary has no idea whether the feeling results from a conjecture produced by a subconscious neuroprocess, or is based on relevant facts embedded in a neuroprocess, or is just a consequence of a neuroprocess that generally induces cautious decision making, or is caused by something else.

Regardless of the case, Mary considers her feeling to be knowledge, as she expresses in the first and last statements.

To sum up: On the one hand, Mary knows "This doesn't work." On the other hand, the statement "This doesn't work" is true, and Mary believes that but cannot justify her belief. Thus we have a counterexample for the claim that knowledge is justified true belief.

The example is just one of a multitude of cases where important parts of asserted knowledge rise as unbidden thoughts from subconscious neuroprocesses, and where the sources justifying these thoughts are untraceable.

This argument doesn't just imply that Plato's definition is wrong. It also indicates that an all-encompassing classification of knowledge as attempted in epistemology—the theory of knowledge—most likely is impossible. Here are the arguments.

At present, epistemology has four core areas of investigation, cited here from the Wikipedia.[117]

- The philosophical analysis of the nature of knowledge and the conditions required for a belief to constitute knowledge, such as truth and justification

- Potential sources of knowledge and justified belief, such as perception, reason, memory, and testimony

- The structure of a body of knowledge or justified belief, including whether all justified beliefs must be derived from justified foundational beliefs or whether justification requires only a coherent set of beliefs

- Philosophical skepticism, which questions the possibility of knowledge, and related problems, such as whether skepticism poses a threat to our ordinary knowledge claims and whether it is possible to refute skeptical arguments

The concepts of belief, perception, reason, memory, testimony, justification, and skepticism implicitly assume that knowledge can somehow be traced as it is acquired, claimed, or used.

In contrast, the neuroprocess hypothesis postulates that neuroprocesses change all the time. One result is that the subconscious neuroprocesses build up and later output untraceable knowledge. This fact impacts each of the above areas and in our opinion makes creation of an all-encompassing theory of knowledge impossible.

How could the work in epistemology proceed? It would be arrogant to suggest an answer. But it seems mandatory that unifying results consider relevant conclusions of neuroscience. We say "unifying results" since at present there are at least 11 schools of thought in epistemology.[118]

In a first step of unification, one could use the conclusions of neuroscience to weed out contradictory philosophical statements.

––––––––––––

Summary: Subconscious neuroprocesses generate feelings and unbidden thoughts whose origin may be untraceable. In such cases, a person cannot justify the knowledge. Hence the claim that knowledge is justified true belief is flawed. We conjecture that this result has further implications for epistemology.

––––––––––––

The exchange between Mary and Peter is an example of a *language game*, a concept invented by Wittgenstein and used by him to great effect to clarify philosophical conundrums. The next chapter covers Wittgenstein's pioneering idea.

13
Language Games

Wittgenstein's *Philosophical Investigations* has a more modest goal than the *Tractatus*. It doesn't attempt to specify what can and cannot ever be said. Instead, it teaches by numerous examples how we can obtain the meaning of language and, with that insight, resolve difficult philosophical questions. Wittgenstein's other posthumously published books have the same goal.

Collectively, the books cover the following areas and topics: aesthetics, certainty, interpretation of color, mathematics, psychology, religious belief, and value. Appendix A includes a brief intuitive discussion that links the *Tractatus* and the *Philosophical Investigations*.

Wittgenstein explains in the *Philosophical Investigations* that we can understand and ultimately resolve a philosophical problem as follows: We invent numerous scenarios that involve the problem and then investigate each scenario in great detail. For a while we live in each scenario, so to speak.[119] He calls each such scenario a *language game* (German *Sprachspiel*). He clarifies that

> "...the term 'language game' is meant to bring into prominence the fact that the speaking of language is part of an activity, or of a life-form."[120]

The detailed investigation of the scenarios clarifies the problem and ultimately resolves it. Wittgenstein states this as follows when we want to understand the meaning of a word.

> "For a *large* class of cases—though not for all—in which we employ the word 'meaning' it can be defined thus: the meaning of a word is its use in the language."[121]

A related comment concerns the essence of things.

> "When philosophers use a word—'knowledge', 'being', 'object', 'I', 'proposition', 'name'—and try to grasp the *essence* of the thing, one must always ask oneself: is the word ever actually used in this way in the language-game which is its original home?—

> "What we do is to bring words back from their metaphysical to their everyday use."[122]

Language games become more powerful when we take the neuro-process hypothesis into account.[123]

Suppose we face a philosophical question. Subconscious neuroprocesses filter and transform the question, and a mixture of feelings and unbidden thoughts accompanies the wording of the question as it enters consciousness.

The feelings may reflect an initial emotional reaction. The unbidden thoughts may include memories of similar instances of the question as well as preconceived notions.

All this happens outside conscious control.

Analysis of the participating subconscious and conscious neuroprocesses then helps clarify the setting. Sometimes we may even identify the answer.

But generally we just have managed to understand the question and are far from answering it. We then create language games as recommended by Wittgenstein: We consciously assemble a large number of situations connected with the problem.

We write down the gist of each game and analyze feelings, unbidden thoughts, and direct actions produced by subconscious neuroprocesses as well as deliberate thoughts, decisions, and actions of conscious neuroprocesses that play a part in the game.

The analysis becomes difficult when the game involves decisions and actions of several persons. For each imagined participant, we consider the results of their subconscious and conscious neuroprocesses.

An example is the language game involving Mary and Peter in Chapter 12. There we analyzed how the output of Mary's subconscious neuroprocesses led to her claim that she knew something.

It can become even more complicated. The neuroprocesses of one person may predict reactions of others. We see examples later when we anticipate how people react to claims about philosophical problems and solutions.

We call the entire process *reflected language* games.[124]

––––––––

Summary: Reflected language games are Wittgenstein's language games enhanced by reflection about the underlying subconscious and conscious neuroprocesses.

––––––––

In subsequent chapters we rely on the neuroprocess hypothesis and reflected language games to resolve long-standing philosophical problems and questions.

14

Never Sure

It is an age-old philosophical question whether we can ever be sure of anything. One answer, described later, refers to the following three types of reasoning.

- Reasoning in mathematics derives theorems from axioms. For example, one defines axioms for the integers $1, 2, 3, \ldots$ and uses them to prove simple theorems such as $1 + 1 = 2$ or more complicated ones such as "The number of prime numbers—the positive integers that aren't the product of two smaller numbers—is infinite."

  The same approach works outside mathematics. One declares some statements to be axioms and uses them to prove statements.

  Regardless of the case, rules of logic govern the proofs. Let's call the process *reasoning from axioms*.

- Somebody claims, "The news is fake because so much of the news is fake."[125] The statement assumes what it claims to prove. This is an instance of *circular reasoning*. In the general case of such reasoning, some assumption is claimed to produce an interesting conclusion when in reality the conclusion is already part of the assumption.

  Circular reasoning is irrelevant in the sense that it doesn't establish anything new or insightful.

- We overhear a discussion.

    Mary: "Electric cars will help us reduce global warming."
    Peter: "How can you be sure?"
    Mary: "I read that in the newspaper."
    Peter: "How would the reporter know?"
    Mary: "She talked with a number of climate specialists."
    Peter: "Where does their knowledge come from?"
    Mary: "They have built mathematical models for the prediction."

    . . .

Suppose Peter is never satisfied with Mary's answers. Then the process goes on and on until Mary gets tired of answering.

Conceptually we can imagine the question and answer process to go on forever. That endless process is called *infinite regress*. It implies that we must *suspend judgment* about the initial claim.

Almost 2,000 years ago, the philosopher Agrippa the Skeptic (1st century) claimed that the proof of any statement can only be accomplished by reasoning from axioms or circular reasoning. In all other cases we must suspend judgment since any proof attempt results in infinite regress. The claim is in the form of a trilemma, that is, it offers three equal solutions. It is called *Agrippa's trilemma*[126] and more recently also *Münchhausen trilemma*.[127]

Let's see what the trilemma means. Suppose we want to prove a statement.

- If it is a case of circular reasoning, the statement is irrelevant. We only need to uncover the circularity.

- If the statement is based on axioms, we may be able to assemble a proof and thus validate the statement.

- If it isn't a case of circular reasoning and there are no axioms, Agrippa declares that we have the infinite regress case and must suspend judgment.

The third case applies to all scientific theories that aren't instances of irrelevant circular reasoning. Since they aren't built on eternally true axioms, we must suspend judgment about the validity of these theories.

———————————

Agrippa assumed—like everybody else at the time—that an input/output machine was the appropriate model for reasoning. Given that viewpoint, the claim makes sense.[128]

Even today it seems difficult to refute Agrippa's claim, though there is a nagging suspicion that something is awry. The neuroprocess hypothesis helps clear up the situation.

According to the hypothesis, a claimed truth—or in modern terminology, a theory—is *never* about the world, for the simple reason that a person's neuroprocesses only know *models* of the world.

For example, take a theory in physics. It is expressed in terms of models that subconscious and conscious neuroprocesses have created.

If the theory is not correct relative to these models, we have a construction error. Upon discovery of such an error, we make suitable corrections. Hence let's assume that the theory is correct in that respect. This implies that the theory will stand as long as the models are not changed.

When the models turn out to be flawed, as for example happened with Newton's model of the universe, all theories resting on those models must be reexamined.

So properly constructed theories do not fail by themselves, but may do so when the underlying models change.

This observation has important consequences for the validation of theories. We shouldn't just see whether a theory has been correctly proved, but should check to what extent the theory is vulnerable to changes in the underlying models. At the very least, we should always be aware of this dependence.

What is the flaw in Agrippa's argument? He assumes that we make statements about the world. This is not the case for anybody, including him. There are only models representing the world, and any claims are about those models.

If we accept the models as a reasonable representation of the world, there is no infinite regress when we try to establish some claim with their aid.

If we succeed and find a proof, fine.

If we don't, we enter a complicated process where we check if we can construct a proof by a suitable addition of models or a change of existing ones. We also may decide to abandon the attempt of proving the claim. That pragmatic process has been going on for tens of thousands of years.

How does Agrippa's skepticism fit into this? The claim makes an incorrect assumption about the world. That is, we do not reason about the world as postulated by the claim, but reason about models of the world. As long as we accept the models, our conclusions are valid. When we change the models, we must revise related conclusions. Seen in that light, the skepticism claim is wrong and should be abandoned.

Summary: The skeptic claims that we cannot ever prove anything and thus must suspend judgment unless we invoke prior axioms or the desired conclusion is part of the assumptions.

The statement would make sense if we were arguing about facts of the world. But the neuroprocesses only know models of the world and not facts. In that scenario the skeptic's claim doesn't apply.

Agrippa's conclusion of suspended judgment turned out to be long-lived. In the next chapter, we see that Popper, whom we first met in Chapter 10, claimed it again in the 20th century.

15

Deduction or Induction

Deduction and induction seemingly are very different processes.

- *Deduction*: We derive a result from given facts, using the rules of logic.
- *Induction*: We guess a new result from a number of samples.

Is the difference between deduction and induction substantive, or is it superficial? Maybe a common process underlies both cases? We look at these questions using the neuroprocess hypothesis.

———————————

We recall from Chapter 10 the following four steps that Popper recommended for the development of scientific theories.[129]

1. Test the proposed theory for internal consistency by comparing its various conclusions.
2. Investigate the logical form of the theory, with the goal of determining whether it is indeed an empirical or scientific theory and not something else, like a tautology.
3. Compare the theory with other theories, mainly to determine whether it constitutes a scientific advance.
4. Test the validity of the theory through empirical application of its conclusions.

We determined in Chapter 10 that the first step, which tests internal consistency of a theory, is a utopian demand.

Here we look at conclusions that Popper develops about the four steps. He views them as a *deductive reasoning* process and contrasts it with *inductive reasoning* for the development of theories, an approach he rejects.[130]

Let's look at his arguments.

In Popper's view, *inductive reasoning* occurs when a collection of events inspires a general theory. If the theory convincingly explains a large number of events, it becomes accepted.

In contrast, he defines *deductive reasoning* to occur when a tentative idea is formulated as a theory, which is then tested. As long as the test results agree with the theory, it remains accepted.

Regardless of the number of successful tests, the theory is never considered proved for the following reason: If at some time the theory fails a test, it has been proved false. This conclusion agrees with the key implication of Agrippa's trilemma of Chapter 14: For any scientific theory, we must always suspend judgment of validity.

Mind you, the above is an oversimplified presentation of Popper's arguments. For example, depending on the situation, he may retain a theory if it passes most tests and fails just a few.

We ignore such subtleties and focus on the two criteria that tell deductive and inductive reasoning apart.

In the inductive case, we see a number of situations and come up with a theory in an inductive leap. In the deductive case, we have an idea, formulate a theory, then verify/falsify the theory by tests.

Differentiating between the two types of reasoning seemingly makes sense. Induction creates a theory from an analysis of events. Deduction puts up a tentative theory that is subjected to verification tests.

Let's look at the two processes under the neuroprocess hypothesis.

In the induction case, some data trigger subconscious neuroprocesses to produce certain feelings and unbidden thoughts. Conscious neuroprocesses build a theory from this information. The second part may—and today often does—involve computational assistance. For example, machine learning methods of artificial intelligence may produce theory candidates.

In the deduction case, subconscious neuroprocesses create feelings and unbidden thoughts that conscious neuroprocesses develop into the idea of a tentative theory. What is the reason for the feelings and unbidden thoughts? The answer is complex, but always involves the following: At some time there must have been some input into or changes of the subconscious neuroprocesses that eventually caused them to output the feelings and unbidden thoughts.

Aren't these two processes very similar? The only difference is in the timing of the data input into subconscious neuroprocesses. We note that our conclusion conflicts with a Wikipedia entry claiming a sharp separation between deduction and induction.[131]

The four steps of theory construction cited at the beginning of this chapter fail to capture the richness and variety of actual events. Here are some of the possibilities.

In the first step, we may ascertain whether somebody else has already proposed or even proved the theory, or we may apply the theory to instances of a well-known collection of situations to get an inkling about its validity. In subsequent steps, we may produce the conjecture of a broadened theory, or validate partial claims of the theory, or link the theory to an entirely different one, or conduct a video conference with a colleague who points out another connection, or find an inconsistency or other error in the theory that prods us to create a modified version, and on and on.[132]

Let us turn to Popper's claim that a theory can never be fully validated and we must always suspend judgment. He says that at best a theory passes a number of tests, and thus may be tentatively accepted. But tomorrow additional tests may surface that show the theory to be wrong.

The proof of Chapter 14 that Agrippa's trilemma is incorrect supports the same conclusion for Popper's claim. Here are the arguments.

- The neuroprocesses construct models to cope with the world and continuously modify them and add new ones. The teaching of elders and reading enhance the learning process.

- We never compare theories with the world, but with the models subconscious and conscious neuroprocesses have created about the world.

- If a theory is not correct relative to these models, we have a construction error. Upon discovery of such an error, we make suitable corrections.

- If a theory is correct relative to the models, it will remain valid as long as we don't change the models.

- When the models turn out to be flawed, as for example happened for Newton's model of the universe, we must reexamine all theories resting on those models.

- As a result, properly constructed theories do not fail by themselves, but may do so when the underlying models change.

- Given these considerations, we should focus on construction errors of theories at hand and possible modifications of models of the world.

- Popper's statement is at odds with that process and should be abandoned.

To what extent are the models of the world created by the neuroprocesses subject to revision?

Some models are so stable that we consider them to be eternally true. For example, nobody doubts that the sun will rise tomorrow. But even those models, seemingly forever valid, may be subject to revision. Just look at the revolutionary change of Newton's universe caused by Einstein's theory of relativity, or consider the impact of quantum physics on our interpretation of very small parts of our world.

As for the daily rising of the sun, we have no idea what the long-term structure of the solar system will be. Every year there are new conjectures about the planets and other bodies of the solar system and their long-term behavior. Wittgenstein anticipated this uncertainty when he wrote:

> "That the sun will rise to-morrow, is an hypothesis; and that means that we do not *know* whether it will rise."[133]

Summary: Deduction and induction seemingly are distinct processes. But when we see them in action, there is much overlap.

The construction of scientific theories is a multifaceted process that defies characterization in a few steps. It always involves models of the world and not facts of the world.

The validity of a theory depends not just on a correct construction but on the validity of the underlying models. The claim that a scientific theory cannot be proved ignores that complexity and should be abandoned.

Newton postulated that gravity causes the elliptical orbits of the planets. He proved the claim with mathematics. How could he be sure that gravity will forever have this effect?

More generally, what is the basis for claims of cause and effect? For 2,400 years philosophers have pondered that question. We take it up in the next chapter.

16

Cause and Effect

Consider the game of billiards. When the cue ball strikes the 8-ball, we know that the 8-ball will move.

When we suffer an infectious disease, we know that our body will fight the invaders.

When we throw a stone into the air, we know that gravity will bend the trajectory and force the stone back onto the ground.

In each case we know the *effect* of some *cause*. What is the basis for this knowledge?

―――――――――――

Philosophers have examined this question since antiquity. We focus on the analysis of David Hume (1711–1776).

He argues as follows:[134]

- Statements of cause and effect are *matters of fact* and cannot be explained as *relations of ideas*.

- Past experiences don't suffice to explain future effects.

The first point is consistent with the above examples. We claim to *know* as a matter of fact that the 8-ball will move, the body will fight the infection, and the stone will fall back onto the ground.

The second point is a postulate about the world.

David Hume.[135]

What is the basis for our knowledge about cause and effect? Hume offers two explanations.

- We have a *custom* or *habit* to convert repeated experiences into expectations about future behavior. Out of habit we declare effects seen many times to be knowledge of cause and effect.

- We have seen the effect so many times that we *believe* it will happen again.

The analysis is different under the neuroprocess hypothesis. The arguments depend on whether a given cause and its effect are solely part of subconscious neuroprocesses, or involve both subconscious and conscious neuroprocesses, or are solely part of conscious neuroprocesses.

––––––––––––––

We start with the first case and look at some examples of cause and effect within subconscious neuroprocesses.[136]

- We build a subconscious neuroprocess for optimal walking speed in thousands of practice walks. Once that neuroprocess is established, the walking speed triggers a feeling of comfortable achievement when optimal speed is selected, and of boredom or discomfort in the nonoptimal case.

- When images are converted to pressure on skin or to electrotactile shocks on the tongue, eventually the person "sees" via the skin or tongue.

- For a deaf person, sound is sometimes converted externally to touch—that is, auditory signals become pressure signals on the skin. After a while, the person "hears" via the skin.

We could extend the list with numerous other examples. Collectively, they demonstrate that subconscious neuroprocesses involve a wealth of cause and effect situations. In each case, the prediction of the effect doesn't rely on conscious beliefs or experiences, but is an intrinsic feature of the neuroprocess.

The case where both subconscious and conscious neuroprocesses are involved is more complicated.

We begin with an actual event.[137] We are on the balcony on the fourth floor of an apartment building and look down on a play area fairly close to the building. A soccer game is in progress.

Now and then the children kick the ball for fun high into the air. We try to estimate the point where the ball will touch the ground again. We think about this very carefully while the ball arcs up and begins to descend. Lo and behold, the ball eventually comes down at a point far away from our estimate.

We repeat this for all subsequent cases. It turns out that for each such trajectory, the accuracy of our estimate is disconcertingly poor. Evidently we cannot improve the performance.

The next day we observe the children again. Time and again, the children kick the ball high into the air, and we estimate the point of touchdown. Each time, we turn out to be wrong and are sorely disappointed by our performance.

In Hume's terminology, we *believe* that the ball will touch down at some point that, it turns out, is very different from the actual one. Moreover, we cannot learn from the experience of the actual touchdown points.

In other words, we may consciously experience effects that are not supported by beliefs. Worse yet, we may not be able to incorporate these effects into our beliefs. The above example and the optical illusions of Chapter 10 are instances.

How is this possible? The answer: Some of our subconscious or conscious neuroprocesses that supposedly are correct for the task actually are inappropriate. These neuroprocesses are of such a fundamental nature that we cannot change them by repeated observations.

Chapter 10 lists the relevant neuroprocesses for two optical illusions. For the trajectory case, we have well established neuroprocesses about objects flying through the air. They were built when we observed numerous times at ground level how objects may rise and descend. The neuroprocesses are so firmly entrenched that observations from an unusually high position cannot modify them.

––––––––––––––

Let's turn to the third case involving just conscious neuroprocesses.

Due to evolution we always search for compact explanations. The original formulation of Occam's razor is a comparatively recent formalization of that goal. Cause and effect are essential concepts for these compact explanations. Model-dependent realism then postulates that the cause and effect explanations of conscious neuroprocesses are facts of the world.

In short: The drive for compact explanations results in the cause and effect claims about the world.

––––––––––––––

Summary: The conflation of neuroprocess output with facts of the world induces the erroneous conclusion that somehow we can find cause and effect in the world and hence should characterize that feature in a philosophical quest.

To the contrary, the cause-and-effect feature of the world is an intrinsic result of the subconscious and conscious neuroprocesses, and philosophical justification, for example with conscious beliefs or experiences, isn't needed or even possible.

In some sense, the neuroprocess hypothesis doesn't just resolve the philosophical question but makes it disappear.

———————————

The next two chapters look at philosophical questions about human vision.

17

Instant Vision

We look at an intriguing question about human vision. How and what do we see with our eyes?

It was posed in the 17th century, triggered extensive discussions over the subsequent 300 years, and was resolved only recently.

Left: William Molyneux.[138]
Right: John Locke.[139]

In 1688, William Molyneux (1656–1698) sent the following letter to John Locke (1632–1704):

"A Man, being born blind, and having a Globe and a Cube, nigh of the same bignes, Committed into his Hands, and being taught or Told, which is Called the Globe, and which the Cube, so as easily to distinguish them by his Touch or Feeling; Then both being taken from Him, and Laid on a Table, Let us suppose his Sight Restored to Him; Whether he Could, by his Sight, and before he touch them, know which is the Globe and which the Cube? Or Whether he Could know by his Sight, before he stretched out His Hand, whether he Could not Reach them, tho they were Removed 20 or 1000 feet from him?"[140]

Molyneux's problem—as it was called shortly thereafter—triggered numerous answers over the next 300 years. The book *Molyneux's Problem* by Marjolein Degenaar[141] examines them in detail.

The author divides the 300 years into four periods.

- The first 40 years, from 1688 to 1728: Since no case of sudden vision was known, philosophical speculation produced a number of "Yes" and "No" answers. Both Molyneux and Locke argued for "No."

- From 1728 to the end of the 18th century: Cataract surgeries produced persons who suddenly became sighted and could be queried about Molyneux's problem. The investigations were inconclusive and resulted in both "Yes" and "No" answers.

- The 19th century: Studies on babies and animals, and scientific advances such as insight into stereoscopic vision, produced additional contradictory answers.

- The 20th century till 1990: Investigations and conclusions were more refined, but did not resolve the problem, either.

The book draws the following conclusion from these puzzling facts.

"The problem had its source in 1688 ... [and] bubbled along a little until ... [a] cataract operation in 1728 ... initiated a flood. The question then quit the high country of philosophy and flowed into the wide plain of experimental psychology and neuropsychology. The mighty stream into which it then flowed has since spread out to form such a wide delta that it is no longer possible to measure its extent."[142]

As the book lays out the multitude of answers, one aspect stands out: Each argument during those 300 years relies on guesses about the vision process. Though the guesses vary, they have one thing in common: Vision is vaguely perceived as a process where visual stimuli produce results.

Key facts established by neuroscience *after* the 300-year period prove that viewpoint to be inadequate.

- Hours, days, weeks, and years after birth, neuroprocesses learn to interpret incoming signals and produce appropriate output. As a result, the person can grab items, interpret images, understand speech, walk, and talk.

- In the case of vision, neuroprocesses accept visual information flowing into the eyes and learn to interpret it as images. During this learning phase, part of the capacity of the brain becomes dedicated to vision.

- If there aren't any visual signals, none of this takes place, and eventually the entire computing capacity of the brain becomes committed to other tasks.[143]

Suppose a congenitally blind person suddenly acquires sight. If that person is very young, maybe just a few months old, then the allocation of the brain's capacity is far from complete, and the above development takes place.

On the other hand, if the person is a teenager or, worse yet, an adult, most or all of the brain's capacity has been committed already, and there is no real estate available, so to speak, where neuroprocesses can deal with the new data.

In the most fortuitous situation, some reallocation of the brain's capacity takes place where other functions yield territory.

In the worst case, such reorganization does not happen, and effective analysis of vision signals never takes place.[144]

The answer to Molyneux's question is therefore:

When a blind person suddenly acquires sight, there are no neuroprocesses available to cope with the visual signals. However, such neuroprocesses may develop. The extent to which this happens depends on several factors: most importantly, the age of the person and the willingness of the person to work hard towards competent vision. It can be a steep, even impossible climb.[145]

The above answer shouldn't be confused with the case where a blind person learns how to see via non-visual clues.[146]

As we have seen in Chapter 3, images may be converted for a blind person to pressure on the skin. After some training, the person "sees" via the skin. When images are converted to electrotactile shocks across the tongue, the person eventually "sees" via the tongue. When images are converted to sound, a person begins to "see" via earbuds.

We close with the report of a congenitally blind person who at age 25 acquired sight in the right eye. It confirms that initially there are no neuroprocesses to understand the vision information.[147]

> "The first two weeks after the operation I saw absolutely nothing, and in order to begin to understand things I touched objects and tried to impress in my mind how they would be without touching them. After about three weeks, I could recognize the letters of the braille alphabet made luminous in a special apparatus ... I became depressed and discouraged when I realized how difficult it was to understand the visual world; in fact all around me I see an ensemble of light and shadow, lines of different length, round and square things, generally like a mosaic of changeable sensations that astonish me, and whose meaning I do not understand."

Later, the person achieved limited processing of vision signals.

> "In newspapers I can read print of 5 mm size, and I can see cars at a 50 m distance. The other day I was able to pick up a knife which had fallen on the floor, also a cigarette, and the soap which had fallen on the bathroom floor. On television I enjoyed watching an ice skating show, following the dark dresses of the dancers against the white of the ice; but I realize that this is only partial vision, and I miss the completeness of full vision."

Summary: For 300 years the limited understanding of the human vision process made it impossible to decide whether sudden acquisition of sight resulted in a visual understanding of the world.

In the terminology of the neuroprocess hypothesis, neuroprocesses for vision must develop in a complex training program before visual input is satisfactorily handled. The development of the neuroprocesses begins after birth. If sight is acquired later, the development becomes progressively more difficult and for older teenagers and adults is almost impossible.

The next chapter examines a theory about vision of the early 19th century.

18

Perception of Color

We hold two color patches side by side. One is yellow, the other red. The yellow seems brighter. If we add a blue patch, the brightness apparently goes down from yellow to red to blue.

Is there a theory of color that covers not only this observation but human perception of color in general?

Johann Wolfgang Goethe.[148]

Johann Wolfgang Goethe (1749–1832)—the most famous German poet—thought so. In an extensive research effort, he created a theory of color that explains human interpretation of and reaction to light and color with a precision reminiscent of mathematics.[149] The theory covers a range of circumstances including colored shadows and refraction of light.

Goethe published the theory in 1810. He considered it his crowning achievement.

> "As to what I have done as a poet, ... I take no pride in it ... But that in my century I am the only person who knows the truth in the difficult science of colours—of that, I say, I am not a little proud, and here I have a consciousness of a superiority to many."[150]

Wittgenstein analyzed Goethe's theory extensively with language games and came to the conclusion that the theory is not valid.[151] We include two of the language games below. They suffice to invalidate Goethe's theory.

───────────────

Wittgenstein demonstrates in the first language game that we may see colors in a picture when there is none.

> "I see in a photograph (not a colour photograph) a man with dark hair and a boy with slicked-back blond hair standing in front of a lathe, which is made in part of castings painted black, and in part of smooth axles, gears, etc., and next to it a grating made of light galvanized wire.

> "I see the finished iron surfaces as iron-coloured, the boy's hair as blond, the grating as zinc-coloured, despite the fact that everything is depicted in lighter and darker tones of the photographic paper."[152]

The converse may occur, too: We may interpret color as black or white. For example, on a chess board with light brown and dark reddish-brown squares, we see several rosewood chess pieces.[153]

Prior to a game of chess, say when comparing the styles and materials of different chess sets, we may declare some pieces to be rosewood colored. But during the game of chess, we call them "black" and not "dark brown" or "rosewood-colored."

Wittgenstein shows in the second language game that our perception of the color of a monochromatic patch depends on the setting. Goethe's theory doesn't account for this fact.

> "Imagine a painting cut up into small, almost monochromatic bits which are then used as pieces in a jig-saw puzzle. Even when such a piece is not monochromatic it should not indicate any three-dimensional shape, but should appear as a flat colour-patch. Only together with the other pieces does it become a bit of blue sky, a shadow, a high-light, transparent or opaque, etc. Do the individual pieces show us the *real colours* of the parts of the picture?"[154]

> "And in this way I think that it is worthless and of no use whatsoever for the understanding of painting to speak of the characteristics of the individual colours. When we do it, we are really only thinking of special uses. That green as the colour of a tablecloth has this, red that effect, does not allow us to draw any conclusions as to their effect in a picture."[155]

A painter relies on the two types of color interpretation described in the language game. While mixing paints and brushing them on the canvas, her perception of colors agrees with the labels on the tubes of paint. When she has applied the paint to the canvas, she steps back and evaluates the added color in the context of the painting.

Let's invoke the neuroprocess hypothesis and move from language games to reflected ones.

There is no guarantee that the subconscious and conscious neuroprocesses handling visual signals, in particular color, are even approximately the same for different people. That's why we must pass a vision test to obtain a driver's license. It assures that we interpret the colors of traffic lights and road signs correctly.

In more sophisticated color tests—for example, during medical exams of pilots—test charts for all possible pairs of colors have different interpretation depending on whether the person can tell the two colors apart.

But even these elaborate tests cannot establish whether a person sees the colors correctly. In fact, the very idea of correct identification of colors is mistaken. It confuses the determination of color frequencies in a laboratory with the processing of colors by subconscious and conscious neuroprocesses.

Wittgenstein's language games cited above already demonstrate that such processing is very different from frequency measurements. But much more can be said about the neuroprocesses. In fact, there is so much material that we cannot include even an overview. For example, there is a significant body of research just investigating how language and culture impact color recognition.[156]

Suffice it to say the following. All these results reinforce the conclusion that Goethe's theory of color is untenable. His work is best seen as a huge intellectual effort that attempts to construct a complete explanation of the perception of colors, and fails.

————————

Summary: Human perception of color defies a simple characterization involving color patches. Even monochrome pictures can induce color. In the language of the neuroprocess hypothesis, complicated neuroprocesses implicitly use a large array of experiences when they evaluate color.

————————

The remaining chapters of this part concern philosophical questions that have been debated for centuries, yet are still considered unresolved.

19

Time

We ask somebody for the time of day, consider some effort a waste of time, respond in a timely manner, may suffer an untimely death, and think about one problem at a time.

We have no trouble understanding the meaning of the word "time" in each case. But what is time itself?

St. Augustine.[157]

In the 4th century, St. Augustine (354–430) pondered this question and concluded that understanding the concept of time was both easy and difficult for him:

"What then is time? If no one asks me, I know what it is. If I wish to explain it to him who asks, I do not know."[158]

1,500 years later, Wittgenstein explains why Augustine has that contradictory experience:

"... This could not be said about a question of natural science ('What is the specific gravity of hydrogen?' for instance). Something that we know when no one asks us, but no longer know when we are supposed to give an account of it, is something that we need to *remind* ourselves of. (And it is obviously something of which for some reason it is difficult to remind oneself.)"[159]

"We feel as if we had to *penetrate* phenomena: our investigation, however, is directed not towards phenomena, but, as one might say, towards the *'possibilities'* of phenomena. We remind ourselves, that is to say, of the *kind of statement* that we make about phenomena. Thus Augustine recalls to mind the different statements that are made about the duration, past, present or future, of events. (These are, of course, not *philosophical* statements about time, the past, the present and the future.)"[160]

What are Wittgenstein's *possibilities of phenomena*? The *phenomena* are situations involving the concept of time, and their *possibilities* are the ways in which the concept is used in these situations. We *remind* ourselves of the possibilities by going over experiences involving the time concept. The experiences may be real or imagined.

What does Wittgenstein mean when he rules out philosophical statements about time? A reasonable answer is that he rejects statements that attempt to say something beyond these experiences.

———————

We rephrase Wittgenstein's advice. When we want to understand the concept of time, we should examine experiences, and nothing else. In particular, we must avoid philosophical arguments that try to say something beyond these experiences. Wittgenstein's explanation of Augustine's conundrum effectively says:

The "If no one asks me ... " part of Augustine's statement covers the situations where the time concept is connected with experiences. Augustine understands that use.

The "If I wish to explain ... " part concerns futile attempts to discuss the time concept outside experiences. Augustine correctly concludes that he cannot accomplish this.

———————

Wittgenstein's advice is consistent with a more general statement by Albert Einstein (1879–1955) about the connection of scientific concepts and experiences.

Albert Einstein.[161]

"We are accustomed to regard as real those sense perceptions which are common to different individuals, and which therefore are, in a measure, impersonal. The natural sciences ... deal with such sense perceptions.

"The conception of physical bodies, in particular of rigid bodies, is a relatively constant complex of such sense perceptions.

"The only justification for our concepts and system of concepts is that they serve to represent the complex of our experiences;

beyond this they have no legitimacy. I am convinced that the philosophers have had a harmful effect upon the progress of scientific thinking in removing certain fundamental concepts from the domain of empiricism, where they are under our control, to the intangible heights of the *a priori*."[162]

We need an abbreviated terminology to simplify statements and declare that a *physics concept* is a concept about the physical world.

Einstein condemns physics concepts at intangible heights since they harm scientific progress. How is this connected with the neuroprocess hypothesis?

The hypothesis says that neuroprocesses build models to understand the world. All physics concepts created that way are based on experiences, in agreement with Einstein's demand.

Physics concepts at intangible heights are beyond anything the neuroprocesses could ever create by looking at the world. Any such concept is irrelevant for understanding the world, indeed cannot be validated, and Occam's razor advises that we drop it.

Here is an example statement involving a physics concept about color at intangible heights.

> The entire world is actually blue. Our neuroprocesses recast this into a variety of colors so that we can understand the world better.

Isn't it amazing that we can comprehend this crazy statement? We could declare it to be—admittedly poor—poetry. But when the statement purports to convey a fact, it doesn't contribute anything to our understanding of the world and should be dropped.

Let's call Einstein's exclusion of physics concepts at intangible heights the *experience rule*. When specialized to the concept of time, the rule evidently is a restatement of Wittgenstein's advice. Physicists indicate their agreement with that conclusion when they say, "Time is what a clock reads."[163]

Philosophers have often violated the experience rule. In particular, the question "What is time?" has been, and still is, answered in a bewildering number of ways.[164]

Before we look at example answers, let's back up the time rule with language games that trace the development of the time concept since the dawn of mankind. In other words, we go over experiences involving the time concept.

One of the earliest uses of time concepts occurs when hunter/gatherers plan what to do next. "Should we hunt today in the forest or in the meadow? Remember that in the past we were successful in the forest." The time concept here is the simple *before* and *after*.

The planning becomes more sophisticated when prey animals undertake yearly treks. In that case, a simple model of the seasons is needed to decide where to hunt. The model connects hunting areas and yearly events of nature such as the blooming of flowers in the spring or the turning of leaves in the fall.

Agriculture calls for more sophisticated models of time. Planting and harvesting must be timed with precision to assure survival. Farmers do so, for example, by identifying the two days of the year when the sun rises at extreme latitudes.

During the past three thousand years, the time models become more and more detailed. For an understanding of the stars' movement, time is measured using years, months, and days. For short-term events, important intervals are hour, minute, and second.

The time concept evidently started with the simple idea of *before*, *after*, and yearly cycles of nature. It then underwent refinement over thousands of years.

Today, we have models using very long time periods, for example in the theory of the Big Bang.[165] Other models involve very short time intervals, for example when the duration of 9,192,631,770 periods of radiation of the cesium 133 atom is used to define 1 second.[166]

Then there is the vast body of scientific theories involving time as a major concept. Einstein's theory of relativity is a pinnacle of these models. It says that elapsed time depends on the speed with which the system containing the clock moves relative to the observer.

———————

So far we have focused on the use of the word "time" where a sequence of events is determined or intervals between events are measured. But there are many other cases where the word is employed in a vague and imprecise way.

When somebody says, "I don't have time for this," it can have a number of interpretations depending on the setting; for example, it may mean "I do not want to be bothered with this."

Other statements using "time" in a vague sense are "She had the time of her life," "You hardly spend any time with me," and "Time is money."

All these examples can be fleshed out and turned into detailed language games. They provide intuitive insight into the complexity and sophistication of the use of "time."

———————

What happens in our neuroprocesses when the time concept is employed? The question can be answered by reflected language games. Here are two examples.

Suppose a certain task typically takes a certain amount of time. Today the going is slow, and we feel pressure that we aren't completing the task by the accustomed time. A subconscious neuroprocess then connects that conclusion about time with a feeling of inadequacy.

The unbidden thought "I wish I had more time for this" may occur in a number of situations. For example, we are in a dead-end job that supplies sufficient income but involves work we are not interested in. On the weekend we discover a passion for painting and lament that we can do this only as a hobby. Complex feelings arise about the way we manage our life. They may even trigger a renewed effort to change jobs.

––––––––––––

Let's turn to the case where the experience rule is violated and the time concept—in Einstein's words—is lifted to intangible heights.[167] Here are four such philosophical claims.

- Philosophical Presentism: Neither the future nor the past exists.[168]
- Growing Block Universe: The past, present, and future exist at the same time.[169]
- The Unreality of Time: Time is unreal.[170]
- Time Reborn: The laws of physics are not fixed, but evolve over time.[171]

We could go on with additional examples, but it would be a boring exercise since the pattern is always the same: The concepts are at intangible heights.[172]

Here is playful advice: Philosophers should give investigations into time that go beyond experiences a time-out.

––––––––––––

Summary: Everybody knows what "time" means in statements based on experiences. Any attempt to go beyond such interpretation results in concepts that, in Einstein's words, are at intangible heights. Reflected language games and the experience rule help us identify such cases.

––––––––––––

The next chapter examines a question that has been answered in a variety of ways for more than 2,000 years.

20

Substance of the World

When we look around, we perceive a multitude of things: galaxies, stars, planets, mountains, rivers, meadows, plants, animals, people, ... The list goes on and on.

In addition, mankind has created many things: cities, roads, bridges, power plants, houses, cars, machinery, ... Here, too, the list seems endless.

The incredible variety of things has motivated philosophers since antiquity to search for a common form, feature, principle, or explanation of the things of the world. The term "substance" is used for all these goals.

Depending on the goal, philosophers have answered the question "What is the substance of the world?" in different ways.[173]

- Pre-Socratic philosophers consider the material of which things consist to be the substance. This statement agrees with today's scientific definition.

- Plato (c. 424–c. 348 BCE) rejects that early claim and instead proposes that something he calls *forms* are the substance. He defines *forms* to be the driving principles that give structure and purpose to everything.

- Aristotle (384–322 BCE) replaces Plato's *forms* with a composite of *form* and *matter*.

As we see in a moment, arguments based on the neuroprocess hypothesis determine the answers of Plato and Aristotle to be nonsensical. That's the reason we don't—in fact, cannot—explain their claims. Similarly we reject almost all subsequent attempts. We include three example cases.[174]

- René Descartes (1596–1650) defines two kinds of substance: *material body* and *mental substance*. The latter term refers approximately to consciousness.
- Gottfried Wilhelm Leibniz (1646–1716) declares that God produced substances continuously by a kind of emanation.
- John Locke (1632–1704) talks about *pure substance in general* and *particular sorts of substance*.

In sharp contrast to the concepts of these and other philosophers, David Hume (1711–1776) says that the belief in substance of the world is the result of a mistake or illusion.

Let's interpret the question "What is the substance of the world?" using neuroprocesses.

As information flows into the body via the five senses, subconscious neuroprocesses handle initial processing, pass feelings and unbidden thoughts to conscious neuroprocesses, and also carry out some direct actions.

Hence our conscious neuroprocesses don't have direct access to the world, which implies that we cannot ever answer the question about the substance of the world.

One might say: We are blind when we try to construct philosophical claims about the substance of the world. This doesn't preclude that our subconscious and conscious neuroprocesses construct sophisticated models of the world.

Chapter 19 contains related comments by Einstein. He advises that we should use concepts and systems of concepts about the physical world solely in connection with experiences and should reject concepts that go beyond. He declares the latter concepts to be at intangible heights.

The concept in this case is *substance*. It has several well-established meanings in the sciences and is also used to express informally that something is important or of a fundamental nature. For example, "This mathematical result is a substantial contribution" means that the result is impressive.

In contrast, the search for a substance of the world as conducted by philosophers over almost 2,500 years has produced concepts at intangible heights. This claim is consistent with Hume's conclusion that the belief in the existence of some such substance is the result of a mistake or illusion.

A related, but easier-to-solve philosophical puzzle is the problem of *universals*.[175]   First formulated by Plato and Aristotle, universals are defined to be qualities or relations common to two or more entities. For example, two sisters have in common that they are human, female, have the same father, and so on. The question is whether universals exist in the world.

The problem was defined when the human mind wasn't considered sophisticated enough to come up with the concept of universals. Hence a postulated prior existence in the real world seemed appropriate.

The difficulty goes away with the neuroprocess hypothesis. Qualities and properties are elementary concepts for subconscious and conscious neuroprocesses and do not deserve independent status as entities of the world.

Summary: The search for a substance of the world, no matter how defined, has produced concepts at intangible heights and thus has been futile.

The question whether universals—that is, qualities or relations common to two or more entities—exist in the world becomes moot under the neuroprocess hypothesis: Universals are elementary concepts of neuroprocesses and not entities of the world.

The next chapter examines a question that doesn't just ask about the substance of the world, but concerns the world's very existence.

21

Realism and Idealism

In the past, somebody may have challenged you with the question "Does a falling tree make a sound if nobody is there to listen?" Strangely enough, no matter how you answered, the questioner proved that your answer was wrong. We see later how this is possible.

The question implicitly involves the link between the world and our perception of it. Since ancient times philosophers have tried to analyze that connection. They created two opposing concepts: realism and idealism.

- *Realism* generally says that the things of the world that we perceive around us exist independently of our perceptions.
- *Idealism* generally declares that what is real is not the world around us. Instead, our perceptions of the world are real.

Answers to the question "Does a falling tree make a sound if nobody is there to listen?" demonstrate the difference between the two viewpoints. The realist answers with "Yes," and the idealist with "No."

Philosophers have investigated many versions of the two positions.[176] As happened in Chapter 20 when we looked at the question about the substance of the world, we don't understand these arguments.

We turn to the neuroprocess hypothesis to see why we cannot comprehend the claims.

The hypothesis talks about the world and the models the subconscious and conscious neuroprocesses build to cope with the world but doesn't claim any reality or non-reality involving the world or the models. Let's see why.

The word "real" has many uses, as we readily see when we construct language games involving that word and related ones.

Consider the following sentences.

> "I am really tired."
> "This economic growth is unreal."
> "You must get real."
> "He lives in an unreal world."
> "This is just another TV reality show."
> "What she is really saying, is . . . "
> "Is this real or just a figment of your imagination?"

The sentences involve "real" in some form. Let's view them as triggers for reflected language games.

When we live in any one of these games, our subconscious and conscious neuroprocesses produce an interpretation of the triggering sentence that most everyone would agree with.

In contrast, when we read the claim "The world is real" or "Our perceptions are real," our subconscious and conscious neuroprocesses don't know what to do with it. Or rather, the subconscious neuroprocesses come up with some vague feelings and unbidden thoughts that conscious neuroprocesses explore with deliberate thoughts. All of these feelings and thoughts are based on everyday use of the world "real."

However, there is no understanding in the way we grasp the meaning of the above sentences. So we give up trying to comprehend the sentences "The world is real" and "Our perceptions are real" and the related claims for or against realism and idealism, and conclude that the statements are nonsensical.

The above analysis of the word "real" is consistent with Wittgenstein's goal:

> "What we do is to bring words back from their metaphysical to their everyday use."[177]

Let's resolve the question "Does a falling tree make a sound if nobody is there to listen?" The word "sound" permits two interpretations: as the sound waves, which the realist claims to exist, and as the perception of them by human ears, which the idealist refers to. If you answer the question with "Yes," you take the position of the realist. The questioner then assumes the role of the idealist to prove you wrong. If you answer "No," the roles are reversed.

So how should you respond? Point out the two interpretations of "sound," and demand that the questioner tell you which case applies. As soon as that is settled, the question becomes a triviality.

Summary: The realist claims that the world is real, while the idealist claims this for the perception of the world. Who is correct? Reflected language games covering the word "real" tell us that both statements are nonsensical.

The related question whether a falling tree makes a sound can be readily resolved when the term "sound" is properly defined.

The concluding chapter of this part deals with a paradox posed in ancient Greece. It was resolved long ago. We include it here as fun reading.

22

Heap Paradox

The Greek philosopher Eubulides (4th century BCE) invented seven paradoxes, among them the following *heap paradox*:

> When you remove one grain from a heap of sand, you still have a heap. But when you continue to do so, eventually nothing is left and there is no heap. At what point does the heap become a non-heap?[178]

The question is puzzling. We vividly imagine the heap and the repeated removal of one grain of sand, see the heap getting smaller and smaller, until nothing is left. But we are unable to identify a point in time where the heap becomes a non-heap. How can we resolve the question?

––––––––––––––––

The meaning of the word "heap" varies, as is evident when we imagine language games involving sentences such as "That did a heap of good," "He earned a heap of money," and "That's quite a heap of food." The statements have in common that the heap is a substantial but unspecified quantity of something physical or imagined.

According to the neuroprocess hypothesis, the concept of heap as an unspecified, large quantity isn't part of the world, but something our subconscious and conscious neuroprocesses have established.

So when a person poses the question "Is this a heap of sand?", they don't expect us to provide a scientific answer, but are asking for an opinion.

Our answer might be, "Yes, there is enough sand to qualify as a heap."

Tomorrow, the same person may ask us the same question about the same pile, and we might respond differently and say, "Looking at the pile again, I am tempted to say that this isn't a heap."

Indeed, we can determine the point where the removal process converts the pile from heap to non-heap only if a heap can be characterized with one-grain precision. The above discussion shows that this is not the case.

Suppose we ignore this insight and actually carry out the reduction process of a heap and remove one grain of sand at a time. We surely say after each of the first few steps, "This is still a heap."

As for the subsequent reduction steps, it is difficult to anticipate our comments. But we can predict how the reduction process will end. At some point, the neuroprocesses will go on strike and output something like "I can't tell if this is still a heap." And then, "You know, this process is really crazy!" At that time, it is clear that the question is nonsensical.

———————

Summary: The philosopher Seneca the Younger (c. 4 BCE–65) captures both the essence and the irrelevance of the heap paradox and other cases invented by Eubulides when he writes:

> "Not to know them [Eubulides's paradoxes] does no harm, and mastering them does no good."[179]

———————

In the preceding chapters we resolved a number of philosophical questions using reflected language games. We use the word "resolved" since we are convinced that our answers are correct. Yet others may claim the answers to be in part or wholly wrong. How can this happen when our conclusions seem irrefutable?

The next part answers the question. The first chapter looks at an unresolved question in mathematics.

Part IV

Limits

23

Invention or Discovery

Chapter 9 argues that mathematicians invent results and don't discover them. Most mathematicians reject that claim and vote for discovery, and comparatively few accept it.[180] In this chapter we trace the conflicting opinions to certain subconscious neuroprocesses. We begin with a story.

———————

In 2013, we were invited to give a talk at a mathematics workshop about the question whether mathematics was invented or discovered. We employed Wittgenstein's concept of language games in the presentation and hoped that the listeners would come to our conclusion.

After the talk many listeners commented that the talk was very interesting. But what was our answer to the question? When we responded with, "Mathematics is invented," there was a moment of polite silence, followed by increasingly heated arguments that we were wrong. "Mathematics is discovered, for sure" was the universal response.

Oh my, we had completely failed. A few years later, in 2017, we completed a book[181] that demonstrates with a large number of language games that mathematics is invented.

We gave talks about the book to groups of mathematicians. Once more there was overwhelming opposition to the conclusion that mathematics is invented. An Internet search of the invention versus discovery question brings up the same contradictory opinions.[182]

Our experience produced a sobering thought: Language games may fail to resolve a philosophical problem. That is, they may supply a solution that is convincing to us but rejected by many people.

———————————

Let's see why one might believe that all mathematical results have always existed somewhere. There are two key points.

First, mathematical education convinces young minds that mathematics is just there, so to speak. The teacher emphasizes rules and doesn't show how important problems motivated the development of methods and results.

Second, mathematicians have been very good at hiding that fundamental concepts are made up. Here is an example.

The natural numbers 1, 2, 3, . . . were invented to fill needs of commerce, as were the four operations of addition, subtraction, multiplication, and division. Then came negative numbers, ratios of these numbers, and so on. But these ideas didn't support proofs for sophisticated developments.

Here is the reason. When we want to prove a statement that applies to *all* possible numbers n, we cannot construct proofs for $n = 1, 2, 3, . . .$ and stop after a while, saying that there is strong evidence that the statement holds for *all* n.

For a valid proof we need something called *induction*. In that procedure, we first prove the statement for an initial *base case*, say $n = 1$. Then in the *inductive step* we assume that the statement is true for an arbitrary n and prove it for the next larger case $n + 1$.[183]

Induction is an indispensable tool for developing mathematics. Yet you cannot find induction anywhere in nature, for the simple reason that you cannot ever observe an infinite collection of things, let alone identify the process of induction for such a collection.

How was induction justified? Something called the *induction axiom* was snuck into the basic definition of the natural numbers.[184] The students absorb this as if it was a fact of nature even though you cannot locate the axiom there.

Many more situations exist where a purely artificial assumption is subtly inserted into a set of axioms and disguised as a most natural thing. An example are the real numbers. Almost all of them require representation with an infinite number of digits.[185]

Once these numbers have been defined, they are manipulated much like the natural numbers and begin to look like something occurring in nature.[186]

All this creates in the mind of the student an orderly world of mathematics that is based on nature, when actually the entire process is artificial and the axioms are pure invention.

The student doesn't absorb this information just at the level of consciousness, but builds it also into subconscious neuroprocesses, just as cognitive behavioral therapy (CBT) predicts. From then on, the student intuitively perceives the induction axiom and real numbers with an infinite number of digits as parts of the world. The term "intuitively" means that there are subconscious neuroprocesses that output that feeling when terms such as "induction" and "real number" are received as input.

Given the axiom-driven teaching of mathematics, these subconscious neuroprocesses get reinforced as mathematical education proceeds and students become mathematicians doing axiom-driven research.

The end result are powerful subconscious neuroprocesses that output positive feelings whenever mathematical results are claimed to exist prior to their development by humans. Given the construction and long-term reinforcement of these neuroprocesses, it's next to impossible to dislodge them with rational arguments. They have become *immutable*. That's the reason even a large collection of language games[187] convinced only a minority of mathematicians that the invention claim is correct.

Will this view change? It's possible.

During much of the 20th century, mathematics was divided into pure and applied mathematics.[188] Pure mathematics focused on the construction of more and more theorems. Applied mathematics used them to solve practical problems. This artificial separation flew in the face of history, where mathematics had been motivated by practical problems.

There has been a shift since the computing revolution of the 1980s. Mathematical development has become a diffuse activity that takes place almost everywhere: in computer science, engineering, the natural sciences, the social sciences, even the arts and humanities.[189]

For example, there is a multidisciplinary effort to develop driverless cars and trucks. We like to view this work as a small step towards methods that endow robots with ingenious thinking—that crazy, often illogical process that turned cave dwellers into outerspace explorers.

We dare claim that most people involved in that effort wouldn't declare that they discover mathematics and then use the information to solve problems. Instead, upon being asked about the role of mathematics, they likely say that they are *developing* mathematics to achieve certain goals. The word "developing" refers to creation and not discovery.

Eventually, these developments may effect a substantial shift of opinion where mathematics is viewed more and more as invention instead of discovery.

Even some of today's axiom-driven research looks more like invention than discovery. A major research effort deals with the concept of infinity. Each of the currently proposed solutions is consistent with prior axioms. In extensive debates mathematicians explore which version should be accepted. The discussion involves terminology such as "construct," "limit conditions on the collections of objects," and "reduce the demands imposed on objects."[190] This looks like an evaluation of inventions, doesn't it?

Summary: Mathematical education depicts the axioms and results of mathematics as if they had a prior existence. The process creates in the students immutable subconscious neuroprocesses that declare mathematics to be discovered and not invented.

Current mathematical developments taking place outside mathematics departments look very much like creation and may induce a shift of view toward invention.

The invention versus discovery question of mathematics is just one instance where a philosophical problem is solved to our satisfaction via reflected language games, yet there is considerable opposition to the conclusion due to immutable subconscious neuroprocesses.

Are such neuroprocesses *always* the root cause when conflicting philosophical opinions cannot be reconciled? The next chapter investigates this question.

24

Immutable Neuroprocesses

Let's use the neuroprocess hypothesis to understand why some philosophical discussions go on forever.

If a philosophical question has been debated for centuries, conscious neuroprocesses of many capable thinkers have addressed the question. Some of their logic arguments may have been faulty. But centuries of effort surely would have identified and eliminated such errors.

Since everybody participating in the debate received the same initial information and we just ruled out persistent reasoning errors of conscious neuroprocesses, the neuroprocess hypothesis allows just one explanation for the endless discussions: The persons processing the philosophical question had different subconscious neuroprocesses that were not affected by the opinions of others. We have called such neuroprocesses *immutable*.

We emphasize that the term is not to imply a positive or negative valuation. It is meant to be neutral. Carl Friedrich Gauss (1777–1855) advocated such valuation humorously.

> "It may be true that men who are mere mathematicians have certain specific shortcomings, but that is not the fault of mathematics, for it is equally true of every other exclusive occupation. So there are *mere* philologists, *mere* jurists, *mere* soldiers, *mere* merchants, etc.

"To such idle talk it might further be added: that whenever a certain exclusive occupation is coupled with specific shortcomings, it is likewise almost certainly divorced from certain other shortcomings."[191]

The explanation that immutable subconscious neuroprocesses cause the interminable debates is a conjecture. Any stronger assertion would be a metaphysical statement, something we want to avoid. But we have found the explanation a useful guide.

Suppose we investigate an endlessly debated philosophical question with reflected language games and find a—for us satisfactory— solution. We compare it with prior, different solutions and search for immutable subconscious neuroprocesses explaining that disagreement. These neuroprocesses provide insight into the reason extensive debates didn't resolve the problem.

Chapter 23 investigates such a case: the endlessly debated question of an invented or discovered mathematics. The search for immutable subconscious neuroprocesses led us to the education in schools and colleges. It plants in the subconscious neuroprocesses of aspiring mathematicians the conviction that mathematics is a part of the world and thus discovered.

The outlook that immutable subconscious neuroprocesses prevent a consensus of answers is depressing. Of course, neuroprocesses may change eventually and eliminate our pessimistic assessment.

Chapter 23 suggests that this may happen for the invention versus discovery question of mathematics. But generally it seems overly optimistic to expect many such changes for problems that have been discussed for centuries.

The outlook is even more dismal for philosophical questions that are purely metaphysical. Examples are "Why does this world exist?" or "What is the property of being?"[192]

These endlessly debated questions seem beyond hope for resolution. The interpretation by subconscious neuroprocesses is almost arbitrary, and current divergent answers are metaphysical speculation.

How is it possible that a person entertains such thoughts?

The subconscious neuroprocesses generally allow for statements of curiosity and dreams of what-might-be, and generally for free-wheeling input. Due to that feature, the neuroprocesses accept fantastic input such as the idea of a multiverse where a group of multiple universes exists.[193] For the same reason, the subconscious neuroprocesses can handle science fiction.

In recent centuries several philosophers—among them Wittgenstein—rejected metaphysical investigations.[194]

The fact that those discussions had no long-term impact demonstrates that the lure of metaphysical speculation is irresistible. That fact also supports the prediction that reflected language games cannot ever be fully successful in weeding out metaphysical speculation—another depressing thought.

Summary: Immutable subconscious neuroprocesses have prevented the resolution of some philosophical problems and likely will continue to do so in the foreseeable future. The outlook is even more dismal for philosophical questions that are purely metaphysical.

Is it possible that a person has *conflicting* immutable subconscious neuroprocesses? The next chapter answers this question.

25

Free Will

Investigations into the question "Do we have free will?" started at least 2,500 years ago and continue today unabated.[195] This chapter lays out why an answer wasn't found during that extensive search and still isn't in sight.

The Wikipedia defines,

> "Free will is the capacity for agents to choose between different possible courses of action unimpeded."[196]

But it doesn't say what "unimpeded" means. Instead, it mentions concepts somehow connected with free will such as moral responsibility, praise, guilt, sin, advice, persuasion, deliberation, and prohibition.

The Stanford Encyclopedia of Philosophy states,

> "The term 'free will' has emerged over the past two millennia as the canonical designator for a significant kind of *control* over one's actions."[197]

It then poses related questions such as,

> "Does [free will] require and do we have the freedom to do otherwise or the power of self-determination?

> "[Is free will] necessary for moral responsibility or human dignity?"[198]

All this means that these excellent sources for information offer only a vague definition of free will. We infer that a precise definition doesn't exist. So how can we possibly answer the question?

In the discussion of the free-will question, our earlier book on models[199] adopts the definition of the Wikipedia using unimpeded actions. This ignores that "unimpeded" isn't properly defined.

The book then describes a number of reflected language games involving decision making with subconscious and conscious neuroprocesses. The games show that a characterization of unimpeded decisions is not possible no matter how "unimpeded" is defined. The book concludes that the question "Do we have free will?" based on the admittedly vague Wikipedia definition is nonsensical.

Let's examine the situation from a different angle where we just look at decision making. Consider a history of events involving a young woman, Sophie.

- Five years ago, suggestive advertising tried to convince Sophie that short hair was important for finding a partner for life. She thought, This doesn't matter, I am not looking.

- Two years ago, Sophie searched for a job. The counselor told her that she would appear to be more professional with short hair. Sophie felt insulted since she considered herself already a professional.

- A year ago, Sophie accepted under hypnosis that she would look better with short hair. She thought, I could have come up with this without paying a hypnotist.

- A month ago, Sophie saw a vintage movie with Audrey Hepburn and thought, I would look like her if I had short hair. When she mentioned this to a friend, she got the response that she would look much older.

- Yesterday, Sophie's mother advised that Sophie would look much more attractive with short hair. Sophie thought, Will Mom's advice ever stop?

- Today, Sophie goes to the hair salon. A short discussion with the stylist triggers an output of related feelings and unbidden thoughts by subconscious neuroprocesses that had evolved over the years. She decides, Hey, I should have my hair cut short.

Does Sophie exercise free will?

Our response: We cannot answer this under any reasonable assumption about the nature of free will. Indeed, the numerous deliberate thoughts and events in the past have impacted a number of subconscious neuroprocesses that participate in today's decision process. There is no way to sort out cause and effect, or dependence or independence.

_____

We could go on and investigate other scenarios where activities create or modify subconscious neuroprocesses and thus lay the groundwork for a decision. Examples are the purchase of a car, the selection of a lifemate, the choice of profession, ... The list goes on and on. In each case, at the moment of choice it is impossible to pinpoint the contribution of the neuroprocesses. Let's look at the cited cases in detail.

- The car decision may be rooted in past experiences with rental cars, frustrating repairs of our current car, the opinion that "I should finally get a car that is more than basic transportation," a comment by a colleague that our car is really kind of old, and a car advertisement that popped up during an Internet search. The aggregate effect may be the purchase decision.

- The decision to search for a permanent partner may come up when we see a happy couple next door who just had a baby, when we experience a sense of loneliness while we look over our shrinking circle of friends, or when we feel with a jolt that it's about time to settle down. Here, too, the multitude of experiences somehow coalesces to the decision to become serious about marrying somebody.

- The choice of profession may be influenced by our mom, in the sense that we may decide we definitely *will never* do what she does, or—alternately—*will do* what she does; by a discussion with a friend who talks enthusiastically about her choice; by an article on the Internet; and by the professor who covered career possibilities. Out of this history rises the idea "I really want to do *this*!"

These arguments show that it is fruitless to ask whether we have free will. From the viewpoint of the neuroprocess hypothesis, decisions are made based on the output of subconscious and conscious neuroprocesses. In turn, changes of these neuroprocesses may have been triggered by so many events that is impossible to point to any one and say, "That's why I am deciding this way."

The question "Do we have free will?" does not consider that convoluted process and thus is nonsensical. If we want to understand why we opt for one decision instead of some alternative, we need to delve into those neuroprocesses as far as possible, consider their history, and—based on that insight—guess why we make the particular choice. For the investigation of subconscious neuroprocesses, techniques of psychotherapy can help.

Given these considerations, we shouldn't attempt to debate presence or absence of free will, or try to classify its manifestations.

Many other people don't feel so constrained, as is evident from the extensive Wikipedia and Stanford Encyclopedia entries.

How is this gulf possible?

In each person, the term "free will" triggers subconscious neuroprocesses connected with various aspects of life: parental guidance, religious upbringing and beliefs, interaction with teachers and other authorities, concerns about moral responsibility and obligations, legal definitions of willful acts, political activities such as voting in a democracy, and on and on.

Let's look at the cited settings.

- Evolution has arranged that children generally follow the guidance of their parents. After all, the parents are an evolutionary success story. Parts of parental advice are inserted into subconscious and conscious neuroprocesses, indeed often define initial versions.

- Religions exploit the fact that children cannot help but accept rules and beliefs. Those rules and beliefs also enter subconscious and conscious neuroprocesses.

- The same goes for teachers and other authorities. They all contribute to the definition of subconscious and conscious neuroprocesses.

Parallel processes emphasize the importance of choices.

- Parents admonish children that they should choose correctly, whatever "correctly" means. The question "What were you thinking?" implies that the child had a choice.

- Some religions emphasize that there are good and bad choices, and that each person must choose correctly. Concepts such as heaven and hell are put up as ultimate destinations to control behavior.

- The legal system could not function without an implied concept of choice and would be engulfed in a chaos of claims "I couldn't help myself."

- The concept of democracy depends on the idea that most citizens vote. Otherwise, small political blocs determine the outcomes.

These two streams of activities are in conflict.

On the one hand, parents, religious leaders, teachers, and other authorities effectively insert into the child important subconscious and conscious neuroprocesses for decision making. Some of the subconscious neuroprocesses are so deeply imbedded that they can't ever be changed and are immutable. That fact is an argument against any version of free will.

On the other hand, the same authorities claim that we have free will to choose. These statements are deeply embedded in another set of immutable subconscious neuroprocesses.

The existence of conflicting neuroprocesses explains the varied responses to the free-will question. Whenever it is posed, subconscious neuroprocesses of the first kind put out feelings and unbidden thoughts that free will is absent, while the output of the second kind of neuroprocesses includes feelings and unbidden thoughts that free will exists.

Each person decides at the spur of the moment which output of the conflicting neuroprocesses is valid. The result is a variety of opinions about free will that depend on who is asked when and where.

It's no wonder that the debate has been going on for centuries and there is no end in sight.

Summary: Some subconscious neuroprocesses involved in choice change continuously as part of life. It is impossible to explain the cumulative effect on decision making.

Other subconscious neuroprocesses for decisions are both immutable and inconsistent.

Given these two facts, it is fruitless to ask whether humans have free will. If we pose the question "Do we have free will?" anyway, we get a random answer depending on whom, when, and where we ask.

––––––––––––––––––

We are at the end of our journey.

Part V

Epilogue

Consider the following three facts about philosophy and neuro-science.

- Philosophy more than any other field of intellectual investigation is not constrained by the world. Almost any concept can be proposed and debated.

  Example topics are covered in the preceding chapters: the origin of ideas, the notion of substance of the world, the claim that reality is a construct, the idea of free will, and so on.

  Let's call the discussion about these and other topics *unfettered debates*.

- Until recently, most everyone viewed reasoning as if performed by an *input/output machine*.

  That concept supported the following belief: The machine may make mistakes, but they can be corrected by rational discussion, and all questions can eventually be answered and all problems solved.

  Let's call this belief *philosophical optimism*.

- Neuroscience has produced considerable insight into the miraculous performance of the nervous system. But the information is far from complete and doesn't suffice for an investigation of unfettered debates and philosophical optimism.

  We characterize this limitation as *neuroscience incompleteness*.

Wittgenstein tried to limit unfettered debates. His contributions are the *Tractatus* and *Philosophical Investigations* plus posthumously published books his students assembled from his notes.

Since he worked in the first half of the 20th century, he—like everybody else at the time—assumed that people deliberated and communicated in a consistent manner.

In our opinion, this assumption is the root cause for the failure of the *Tractatus*, as discussed in Chapter 11.

The *Philosophical Investigations* didn't suffer the same fate. In fact, the book proposes a method of philosophical investigation—*language games*—that uses neuroprocesses as a simulator. In these games we immerse ourselves into imagined situations and observe the neuroprocesses. Of course, the observations extend only to the conscious neuroprocesses, and we experience the subconscious neuroprocesses indirectly by seeing their output but not their reasoning.

As neuroscience proceeds, we expect that the simulator concept will become more and more powerful. This is the long-term view. But current neuroscience results are too incomplete to impact language games significantly. We overcome this limitation by introducing the *neuroprocess hypothesis*. It postulates key features of the subconscious and conscious neuroprocesses.

Reflected language games use the hypothesis to expand the role of Wittgenstein's language games.

The neuroprocess hypothesis and reflected language games are two key tools for our investigation of philosophical problems.

———————

When we began philosophical investigations with the two tools, we put up the following goals.

- Demonstrate that the two tools support the solution of long-standing philosophical problems and thus can help stop unfettered debates.

- Explain with the two tools why some problems haven't been solved and likely won't be solved in the foreseeable future—in contrast to the expectation of philosophical optimism.

To what extent have we reached those goals? That's not for us to say, but for you, the reader, to decide.

Appendix A: Two Questions

Two questions connect Wittgenstein's *Tractatus* and *Philosophical Investigations*.

We start out and imagine that metaphysical claims prompt Wittgenstein in the 1910s to consider the following question: "Why do metaphysical statements arise?" In the *Tractatus* he supplies an answer. As described in Chapter 11, he constructs logical atomism and the picture theory to establish limits on language. With these two tools, he determines what can and cannot be said. The "cannot" part includes all metaphysical statements.

While developing the two theories, he realizes that his construction involves metaphysical claims. He eliminates the problem with a ladder argument—which is another metaphysical statement!

In the second part of the 1920s, he realizes that the *Tractatus* not only eliminates all metaphysical statements, but also legitimate communication. There is no way to repair this structural defect.

In response, he abandons the *Tractatus* and focuses on a simpler question: "How can metaphysical statements be avoided?" He supplies language games as key tool in the *Philosophical Investigations*. That approach avoids any criticism of metaphysical construction.

Here is the interesting way the two, very different, solutions are connected. In Chapter 6 of the *Tractatus*, Wittgenstein arrives at strong conclusions ruling out metaphysical statements.[200] The final

Chapter 7 consists of one sentence that sums up those thoughts. It still is frequently quoted even though its proof relies on the defective logical atomism and picture theory.

"What we cannot speak about we must pass over in silence."[201]

Why have people been fascinated by this statement?

Our answer: His rejection of metaphysical statements resonates with many people and likely will do so in the future.

In the *Philosophical Investigations* Wittgenstein abandons the absolute statements of the *Tractatus* and says that he

"... bring[s] words back from their metaphysical to their everyday use."[202]

As shown in Part IV, there are limits for the effectiveness of language games that cannot be overcome. Wittgenstein may have sensed these limits when he writes in the preface of the *Philosophical Investigations*:

"I should have liked to produce a good book. This has not come about, but the time is past in which I could improve it."[203]

We shouldn't be misled by this comment. The *Philosophical Investigations* is a meticulously assembled description and analysis of a multitude of language games.

But evidently Wittgenstein aimed for more: a well-ordered description of language games spanning the vast range of human thought. But given the richness of human experience, this isn't possible.

Notes

Throughout, "Wikipedia" refers to the English version. All sources and links were accessed for final verification in June 2022.

Chapter 1 Introduction

1. See Wikipedia "Free will," "Knowledge," and "Time."

2. It is interesting that each philosopher considered his thinking to be correct but that others could make mistakes. This is captured by the input/output machine model: The machine doesn't produce self-doubt.
It may seem that the thinking of the skeptic is different. But the skeptic is *sure* of not knowing something; see Wikipedia "Skepticism."

3. Plato (c. 424–c. 348 BCE) claimed that the heart carried out reasoning, Galen (129–c. 210) postulated the brain as location, and René Descartes (1596–1650) assigned thinking to the mind. Given today's insight into the functioning of the human body, thinking cannot be assigned to a specific organ or location.
See Wikipedia "Cardiocentric hypothesis," "Galen," "René Descartes," and [Bennett and Hacker, 2003].

4. See Wikipedia "'Nervous system" and "Outline of the human nervous system."

5. [Grafton, 2020].

6. [Damasio, 2021].

7. [Bennett and Hacker, 2003] and [Hacker, 2019] stress that persons, and not brains, think. See also [Bennett et al., 2007].

8. For early ideas about neuroprocesses connecting persons with the world, see Wikipedia "Unconscious interference" and "Embodied cognition." [Edgar, 2015] examines relevant results of the 19th century in detail.

9. See Wikipedia "Hermann von Helmholtz."

10. See Wikipedia "Euclidean geometry" and "Non-Euclidean geometry."

11. See Wikipedia "Theory of relativity."

12. See Wikipedia "Deism" and "Atheism."

13. The Stanford Encyclopedia of Philosophy "The Philosophy of Neuroscience" has more than 17,000 words.

Chapter 2 Interaction with the World

14. [Kepler, 1627].

15. See Wikipedia "Orbit," "List of future astronomical events,"and "Timeline of the far future."

16. [Hawking and Mlodinow, 2010].

17. For example, we can share with others the visual impression of a house in the following sense. When we talk about the house, we know that others have the same or similar sense impression. But when we prick a finger, we cannot share the feeling of pain.

18. Source: "Stephen Hawking" by NASA - Original. StarChild Learning Center. Archived directory listing. Public Domain, https://commons.wikimedia.org/w/index.php?curid=1657641. Cropped photo.

Chapter 3 Results of Neuroscience

19. See Wikipedia "Outline of the human nervous system."

20. [Eagleman, 2020].

21. Source: "Nervous system diagram." By Medium69, Jmarchn, CC BY-SA 4.0 https://creativecommons.org/licenses/by-sa/4.0, via Wikimedia Commons.

22. Chapters 1 and 4 [Eagleman, 2020].

23. See Wikipedia "Direct acoustic cochlear implant."

Chapter 4 Fatigue

24. Chapter 4 [Truemper, 2021] supplies part of the material of this chapter.

25. Craig Glenday, Editor-in-Chief at Guinness World Records, reports on https://www.quora.com/What-is-the-longest-distance-a-person-has-walked-in-one-go:
"Georges Holtyzer of Belgium walked 673.48 km (418.49 miles) in 6 days 10 hr 58 min, completing 452 laps of a 1.49 km (0.92 mile) circuit at Ninove, Belgium, from July 19 to July 25, 1986. He was not permitted any stops for rest and was moving 98.78 percent of the time."

26. p. 209 [Grafton, 2020].

27. p. 210, 211 [Grafton, 2020].

28. p. 213 [Grafton, 2020].

Chapter 5 Neuroprocess Hypothesis

29. See Wikipedia "Paavo Nurmi."

30. p. 214 [Grafton, 2020].

31. [Gibson et al., 2013] describes three stages of collapse.

- During the early stage—the "Early Foster" collapse position— the runner exhibits unstable gait and lowers the head.
- The gait deteriorates to a shuffle in the "Half Foster" collapse position, with head parallel to the ground.
- In the final stage—the "Full Foster" collapse position—the runner crawls on the ground on elbows and knees and finally collapses before or after reaching the finish line.

The reference conjectures that the collapse positions are indicative of a final, likely primordial, protective mechanism.

32. [Burns, 2020] provides not only a clear introduction, but is sufficiently detailed for readers who are looking for solutions they can implement by themselves.

33. See Wikipedia "Cognitive behavioral therapy." For treatment

examples, see [Beck et al., 1979], [Burns, 2008], and [Burns, 2020]. [Truemper, 2021] describes a composite case.

34. See Wikipedia "Preferred walking speed." The total energy consumption per mile is called *gross cost of transport*.

35. [Selinger et al., 2015]. See also p. 192 [Grafton, 2020] and the section on Energetics of Wikipedia "Preferred walking speed." [Truemper, 2021] compares the process with the difficult computation of optimal glide speed for airplanes.

Chapter 6 Justification

36. See Wikipedia "Grid cell," "Place cell," and "Head-direction cell." To learn more about the discoverers of these cells, see Wikipedia "Edvard Moser, "John O'Keefe (neuroscientist)," and "James B. Ranck Jr."

37. [Zacks, 2020].

38. [Eagleman, 2020].

39. [Grafton, 2020].

40. [Mlodinow, 2022].

41. [Damasio, 2021].

42. [Nestor, 2020].

43. Chapter 5 [Truemper, 2021] has details using the terminology of models instead of neuroprocesses.

44. [Kahneman, 2011].

45. [Kabat-Zinn, 1990].

46. [Truemper, 2021].

47. See `http://www.nasonline.org/programs/nas-colloquia/com pleted_colloquia/brain-produces-mind-by.html`.

48. [Conant and Ashby, 1970] establishes that every good regulator of a system must be a model of that system. The stated claim about the brain is a corollary.

Chapter 7 Summary

49. See Chapter 1.

50. See Chapter 4.

51. See Chapter 5.

Chapter 8 The Platonic World

52. Copy of the portrait made by Silanion c. 370 BCE for the Academia in Athens. From the sacred area in Largo Argentina. Source: https://en.wikipedia.org/wiki/Plato#/media/File:Plato_Silanion_Musei_Capitolini_MC1377.jpg. By English: Copy of Silanion - Marie-Lan Nguyen (User:Jastrow) 2009. Licensed under CC BY 2.5 via Commons.

53. See Wikipedia "Theory of forms."

54. See Stanford Encyclopedia of Philosophy "Plato."

55. See Wikipedia "Theory of forms."

56. See Wikipedia "Cardiocentric hypothesis."

57. See Wikipedia "Galen."

58. See Wikipedia "2001: A Space Odyssey (film)."

59. See Chapter 4.

60. Chapter 6 [Truemper, 2021].

61. See Wikipedia "Piano Concerto No. 3 (Rachmaninoff)" and search the Internet for "number of notes in rachmaninoff piano concerto number 3." The cited count assumes that the pianist plays the ossia cadenza.

62. [Gladwell, 2005].

63. See Wikipedia "Conceptual space" and [Gärdenfors, 2004].

64. See Wikipedia "Neuroesthetics."

65. See Chapter 6.

66. [Eagleman, 2020] and [Grafton, 2020] provide excellent overviews.

67. See Wikipedia "Occam's razor."

68. See Stanford Encyclopedia of Philosophy "Logical Constructions."

69. See Wikipedia "Aether theories."

70. See Wikipedia "Michelson-Morley experiment."

Chapter 9 Natural, Discovered Mathematics

71. See Wikipedia "Philosophy of Mathematics." It summarizes
pros and cons for numerous claims about the nature of mathematics.

72. See Wikipedia "Philosophy of mathematics."

73. [Wigner, 1960] and [Hamming, 1980].

74. [Abbott, 2013].

75. p. 138 [Kaku, 2021] cites a glaring example: When the amount
of dark energy in the universe is computed under the assumption
of relativity and quantum theory, the resulting value is 10^{120} times
larger than the currently accepted value. Written in decimal nota-
tion, the factor is a 1 followed by 120 zeros.

76. See [Rudman, 2007] and Wikipedia "History of mathematics"
for details about this complicated process.

77. See, for example, the key papers of mathematical developments
assembled in [Newman, 1956] or the discussion of the start of mathematics in [Rudman, 2007]. [Truemper, 2017] focuses on the strug-
gle of mathematicians for clarity.

78. See Wikipedia "Formation and evolution of the Solar System."

79. In the key arguments of calculus, Newton divides a quantity
$f(x+d) - f(x)$ by a positive value d. Shortly thereafter, he declares
$d = 0$. But then the earlier step involved division by 0, which is not
allowed!
Below is Newton's justification, cited on p. 9 [Cajori, 1919]:
"It is objected, that there is no ultimate proportion of evanescent
quantities [here, $f(x+d) - f(x)$ and d are the evanescent quanti-
ties]; because the proportion, before the quantities have vanished,
is not ultimate; and when they have vanished, is none. But, by the

same argument, it might as well be maintained, that there is no ultimate velocity of a body arriving at a certain place, when its motion is ended: because the velocity, before the body arrives at the place, is not its ultimate velocity; when it has arrived, is none.

"But the answer is easy: for the ultimate velocity is meant that, with which the body is moved, neither before it arrives at its last place, when the motion ceases, nor after; but at the very instant when it arrives; that is, the very velocity with which the body arrives at its last place, when the motion ceases.

"And, in like manner, by the ultimate ratio of evanescent quantities is to be understood the ratio of the quantities, not before they vanish, nor after, but that with which they vanish."

Why is this analogy wrong? When the arrow hits the target, the velocity does not instantaneously drop from a given value to 0. If that were so, the arrow would hit the target with infinite force. Hence the image of an arrow hitting a target is misleading.

Bernard Bolzano (1781–1848), Augustin-Louis Cauchy (1789–1857), and Karl Weierstrass (1815–1897) eliminated the conflict in Newton's proof more than 150 years later, using the concept of function continuity; for example, see [Truemper, 2017].

80. See Wikipedia "Axiom of choice."

81. See Wikipedia "Banach-Tarski paradox."

82. See Wikipedia "Brouwer-Hilbert controversy."

83. See Wikipedia "Axiom of choice."

84. [Livio, 2009] claims an in-between case: The axioms of mathematics are invented, but as soon as any one of them is in existence, so are all results that can now be deduced.

This claim flies in the face of mathematical history. For example, when Georg Cantor (1845–1918) claimed in [Cantor, 1895] that every infinite set contains the set of integers as a subset, he couldn't possibly supply a correct proof since certain axioms, such as the axiom of countable choice, hadn't been invented yet. For details about this axiom, see Wikipedia "Axiom of countable choice." Hence Cantor couldn't possibly have discovered the result and must have invented it.

85. See Wikipedia "Borwein's algorithm."

86. See Wikipedia "Bailey-Borwein-Plouffe formula."

87. The cited breakthroughs for the computation of π have trig-

gered a worldwide competition. A massive computing effort has established π with ever increasing precision. In 2021, the record was more than 50 trillion ($= 50,000,000,000,000$) digits. For the most recent result, search the Internet for "largest number of digits of pi ever computed."

88. [Théra, 2017].

89. [Lakatos, 2015].

90. Source: " Jonathan Borwein" photo by Mark Graham. Copyright held by APM Institute for the Advancement of Physics and Mathematics, Athens, Greece. The institute kindly granted permission to use the photo.

91. [Wolfram, 2013].

92. Source: "Stephen Wolfram" photo by Stephen Wolfram's PR team/Stephen Faust - Received via email from Stephen Wolfram's staff, Creative Commons BY-SA 3.0, https://commons.wikimedia. org/w/index.php?curid=99960643.

93. [Wolfram, 2022].

Chapter 10 Consistency

94. Source: "Popper in 1990" by Lucinda Douglas-Menzies. No restrictions. https://en.wikipedia.org/wiki/Karl_Popper#/media/F ile:Karl_Popper2.jpg. Cropped photo.

95. p. 9 [Popper, 1992].

96. For any X and Y, the statement "X implies Y" is true if, for each possible case, X is false or Y is true. Since "A, B, and C" is always false, the statement "A, B, and C imply S" is always true, and S is indeed a conclusion of the theory.

97. See Wikipedia "Kurt Gödel."

98. See Wikipedia "Schrödinger's cat."

99. See Wikipedia "Quantum entanglement."

100. pp. 10–13 [Truemper, 2021].

101. Wikipedia "Checker shadow illusion." By Edward H. Adelson, own work, and vectorized by Pbroks13. https://en.wikipedia.o

rg/wiki/Checker_shadow_illusion#/media/File:Checker_shadow_i
llusion.svg. Licensed under CC BY-SA 4.0 via Commons.

102. Wikipedia "Checker shadow illusion." By Edward H. Adelson, own work, and vectorized by Pbroks13. https://en.wikipedia.o rg/wiki/Checker_shadow_illusion#/media/File:Grey_square_opti cal_illusion_proof2.svg. Licensed under CC BY-SA 4.0 via Commons.

103. Source: "Shepard tables illusion." By tables - Own work, CC BY-SA 4.0, https://commons.wikimedia.org/w/index.php?curid= 64967958.

104. Source: "Surfaces of Shepard tables." Extracted by K. Truemper from work by tables, CC BY-SA 4.0, https://commons.wikime dia.org/w/index.php?curid=64967958.

105. See Wikipedia "Shepard tables" for details about this amazing construction by Roger N. Shepard.

106. A letter of Gauss to F. Taurinus includes the following philosophical statement, see p. 250 [Engel and Stäckel, 1895]: "... All efforts of mine to find a contradiction, an inconsistency in this non-Euclidean geometry have been fruitless, and the only thing that makes our brain resist it [the geometry], is that, if true, there would have to be a certain (though not known by us) constant of linearity. But I think that, despite the vacuous word-wisdom of the metaphysicists, we know not enough or indeed nothing about the true nature of space, that we can permit us to confuse something that appears to us unnatural with something that is absolutely impossible. If the Euclidean geometry was the true one, and the constant [used in the non-Euclidean geometry] was related to values that could be measured on earth or up in the sky, then we could determine the true nature [of space] *a posteriori*. So jokingly I have sometimes expressed the wish that the Euclidean geometry was not the true one, since then we would have an absolute measure [of the constant] a priori."

107. See Wikipedia "Eugenio Beltrami."

108. See Wikipedia "Tarski's axioms."

Chapter 11 Tractatus Logico-Philosophicus

109. [Wittgenstein, 1963].

110. [Wittgenstein, 1958].

111. Source: "Ludwig Wittgenstein" by Moritz Nähr - Austrian National Library. https://en.wikipedia.org/wiki/Ludwig_Wittgenstein#/media/File:Ludwig_Wittgenstein.jpg. Public Domain under US copyright code PD-old-70.

112. Preface [Wittgenstein, 1958].

113. In 1930, Wittgenstein included in his notes a harsh critique of the ladder argument; see Wikipedia "Wittgenstein's ladder":
"I might say: if the place I want to get [to] could only be reached by way of a ladder, I would give up trying to get there. For the place I really have to get to is a place I must already be at now.
"Anything that I might reach by climbing a ladder does not interest me."

114. Rebecca Saxe tells how the neuroprocesses simulate what other people are thinking, in her presentation "How the Brain Invents the Mind," YouTube video https://www.youtube.com/watch?v=Wn0PzB-iv5o, delivered at the National Academy of Sciences colloquium "The Brain Produces Mind by Modeling," 2019.

Chapter 12 Knowledge = Justified True Belief

115. See "Gettier problem" in Wikipedia "List of unsolved problems in philosophy."

116. See Wikipedia "Belief."

117. See Wikipedia "Epistemology."

118. See Wikipedia "Epistemology."

Chapter 13 Language Games

119. Chapter 14 [Truemper, 2021] contains a fully worked out example where the concept of quality is investigated.

120. Paragraph 23 [Wittgenstein, 1958].

121. Paragraph 43 [Wittgenstein, 1958].

122. Paragraph 116 [Wittgenstein, 1958].

123. Wittgenstein considers consciousness in a variety of settings in

the *Philosophical Investigations*, but only in the sense of self-aware-ness. Just search the *Philosophical Investigations* for "consciousness" and verify that the word is used each time in the sense of self-awareness. This implies that Wittgenstein didn't think about any-thing like subconscious neuroprocesses. That's not surprising, given the results of neuroscience available at that time.

124. In [Truemper, 2021] we called the entire process *Wittgenstein's method*. We now prefer *reflected language games* since it points to Wittgenstein's language games and the reflection involving sub-conscious and conscious neuroprocesses.

Chapter 14 Never Sure

125. US President D. Trump during news conference, February 16, 2017. See https://www.cnn.com/2017/02/16/politics/donald-trump-press-conference-amazing-day-in-history/index.html.

126. See Wikipedia "Agrippa the Sceptic." Five arguments, called the five *modes* of Agrippa, are the foundation for his conclusion.

• *Dissent*: The differences of opinions among philosophers and people in general demonstrate uncertainty of claims.

• *Progress ad infinitum*: Each proof of a claim rests on matters re-quiring proof themselves. Hence an infinite progression of proofs is needed.

• *Relation*: All things change whenever their relationships change, or as we consider them from different angles.

• *Assumption*: The asserted truth rests on unproven assumptions.

• *Circularity*: The asserted truth involves circularity of arguments, where what is to be proved is actually assumed.

The first and third points—*Dissent* and *Relation*—are just observa-tions. But the other three claims—*Progress ad infinitum*, *Assumption*, and *Circularity*—are philosophical conclusions. We use the terms *infinite regress* (= Progress ad infinitum), *reasoning from axioms* (= Assumptions), and *circular reasoning* (= Circularity).

127. See Wikipedia "Münchhausen trilemma."

128. Let's try and intuitively justify Agrippa's trilemma. Imagine we want to prove a claim. We consider consequences when the claim is assumed to be false. If that leads to a contradictory result, we know that the claim is true.

When we have axioms, there is the possibility that we find a contradiction involving one or more of the axioms. But if there are no axioms, how can we hope to assemble a contradiction? Agrippa felt that if we do find a contradiction in the absence of axioms, it's just a case of circular reasoning. So in the absence of circular reasoning, he argued that the search for a contradiction never terminates and we have infinite regress. As a consequence, we must suspend judgment.

Chapter 15 Deduction or Induction

129. p. 9 [Popper, 1992].

130. p. 9, 10 [Popper, 1992].

131. Is it always possible to sharply separate induction and deduction, or are there cases where we cannot tell the difference?
Wikipedia "Inductive reasoning" claims that there is a sharply defined difference:
"Inductive reasoning is a method of reasoning in which a body of observations is synthesized to come up with a general principle. *Inductive reasoning is distinct from deductive reasoning*. If the premises are correct, the conclusion of a deductive argument is certain; in contrast, the truth of the conclusion of an inductive argument is probable, based upon the evidence given." [emphasis added]
We have some questions about this definition. What is the synthesis process of induction? Can't it involve deduction from the given observations? Since we may have unavoidable deduction errors—for example, due to imprecision of data—shouldn't the definition of induction versus deduction be independent of the accuracy of the result? How about machine learning of artificial intelligence? Its methods often use deduction to analyze data, then assemble the results to an inductive claim. For example, a deductive analysis of medical symptom data may reveal relationships that we reinterpret as new inductive insight into diagnosis. Isn't the deductive part of the method *designed* to produce that inductive insight?
Given these troubling questions, it seems best to be pragmatic about the use of the two terms.

132. [Lakatos, 2015] provides a beautiful demonstration of the process where a teacher guides a class of students in the construction of a theorem of geometry. The numerous steps involve arguments, counterarguments, wrong theorems, wrong proofs, and reformulations. It's a messy process. But eventually it produces the desired

theorem with a correct proof.

133. Paragraph 6.36311 [Wittgenstein, 1963].

Chapter 16 Cause and Effect

134. The summary of Hume's work is based on the detailed discussion of Hume's investigation into cause and effect in Stanford Encyclopedia of Philosophy "David Hume." For a complete list of entries about the cause-and-effect question in that encyclopedia, search in that encyclopedia with the key word "causation." It brings up more than 500 entries.

135. Source: "David Hume." by Allan Ramsay. Scottish National Portrait Gallery. Public Domain, https://commons.wikimedia.org/w/index.php?curid=1367760.

136. Chapters 3, 4, and 5 have details about the cited examples.

137. We observed the process ourselves years ago and confirmed that a friend had exactly the same reactions.

Chapter 17 Instant Vision

138. Source: "William Molyneux." Attributed to Sir Godfrey Kneller, Bt - National Portrait Gallery http://www.npgprints.com/image/20967/sir-godfrey-kneller-bt-william-molyneux, Public Domain. https://commons.wikimedia.org/w/index.php?curid=27456780.

139. "Portrait of John Locke by Sir Godfrey Kneller (1697)." By Godfrey Kneller - 1. Unknown source 2. derivate work of File:Godfrey Kneller - Portrait of John Locke (Hermitage).jpg of arthermitage.org, Public Domain, https://commons.wikimedia.org/w/index.php?curid=110128.

140. p. 17 [Degenaar, 1996]. The preamble of the book contains a photocopy of the letter.

141. [Degenaar, 1996] is based on the doctoral dissertation the author completed in 1992, which is about 300 years after Molyneux posed the problem in 1688.

142. p. 133 [Degenaar, 1996].

143. Chapter 8 [Eagleman, 2020] explains that the brain has *limited*

real estate and that the entire brain is used for the diverse tasks.

144. [Barry, 2021] describes in detail the learning process for vision. Each aspect is illustrated with the learning experience of a child who was legally blind till age 15.
On pp. 201–214, the book eloquently discusses the plasticity of the brain for reallocation of computing capacity.

145. [Barry, 2021] describes a number of cases where people couldn't accomplish the steep climb to effective vision, but also tells of success stories.
Project Prakash is an organization based in the United States that provides treatment for blind children in India. Studies conducted in connection with that work confirm the conclusion that age is the most critical factor for establishing vision. See `https://www.projec tprakash.org/`.

146. Chapter 4 [Eagleman, 2020].

147. p. 39 [Valvo, 2014].

Chapter 18 Perception of Color

148. Source: "Johann Wolfgang Goethe." By Joseph Karl Stieler, 1828, detail. `https://en.wikipedia.org/wiki/Johann_Wolfgang_vo n_Goethe#/media/File:Goethe_(Stieler_1828).jpg`.
Transferred from nds.wikipedia to Commons by G. Meiners 2005. Public Domain.

149. [Goethe, 1810] has the details of Goethe's theory of color. See also Wikipedia "Theory of Colours" and Chapter 9 [Truemper, 2017].

150. p. 302 [Oxenford, 1930].

151. [Wittgenstein, 1978].

152. Part I, paragraph 63 [Wittgenstein, 1978].

153. Chapter 9 [Truemper, 2017].

154. Paragraph 60 [Wittgenstein, 1978].

155. Paragraph 213 [Wittgenstein, 1978].

156. See Wikipedia "Color term" and "Linguistic relativity and the color naming debate."

Chapter 19 Time

157. "St. Augustine in His Study." By Sandro Botticelli, 1494 - Botticelli: de Laurent le Magnifique à Savonarole: catalogue de l'exposition à Paris, Musée du Luxembourg, du 1er octobre 2003 au 22 février 2004 et à Florence, Palazzo Strozzi, du 10 mars au 11 juillet 2004. Milan: Skira editore, Paris: Musée du Luxembourg, 2003. ISBN 9788884915641, Public Domain, `https://commons.wiki media.org/w/index.php?curid=12076672`.

158. Book XI, Chapter IV [Augustine, 400].

159. Paragraph 89 [Wittgenstein, 1958].

160. Paragraph 90 [Wittgenstein, 1958].

161. Source: `https://en.wikipedia.org/wiki/Albert_Einstein#/m edia/File:Albert_Einstein_%28Nobel%29.png`. "Albert Einstein (Nobel)" by Unknown - Official 1921 Nobel Prize in Physics photograph. Licensed under Public Domain via Commons.

162. [Einstein, 2003].

163. See Wikipedia "Time in Physics."

164. The "Time" entries of the Wikipedia and Stanford Encyclopedia of Philosophy discuss the time concept as it has evolved over thousands of years. See also Wikipedia "Eternalism (philosophy of time)."

165. See Wikipedia "Big Bang."

166. See Wikipedia "Second."

167. See Wikipedia "Time" and "Eternalism (philosophy of time)," and Stanford Encyclopedia of Philosophy "Time."

168. See Wikipedia "Philosophical presentism."

169. See Wikipedia "Growing block universe."

170. See Wikipedia "The Unreality of Time."

171. See Wikipedia "Time Reborn."

172. See also several modern contradictory theories of time cited in [Grötschel, 2020]. Each of the time concepts resides at intangible

heights.

Chapter 20 Substance of the World

173. See the "Substance" entries in the Stanford Encyclopedia of Philosophy and the Wikipedia.

174. See Stanford Encyclopedia of Philosophy "Substance."

175. See Wikipedia "Problem of universals."

Chapter 21 Realism and Idealism

176. See Wikipedia "Philosophical realism" and "Idealism" for extensive coverage of the versions of realism and idealism.

177. Paragraph 116 [Wittgenstein, 1958].

Chapter 22 Heap Paradox

178. See Wikipedia "Eubulides." The heap paradox is also known as the *sorites paradox*.

179. See Wikipedia "Eubulides" for this comment by Seneca the Younger and evaluations by other philosophers.

Chapter 23 Invention or Discovery

180. [Truemper, 2017].

181. [Truemper, 2017].

182. In May 2022, the Internet query "invention or discovery of mathematics" produced more than 24 million entries arguing for invention or discovery.

183. There is an equivalent process where we also prove the base case, but then assume that the statement is false for some larger n. Then it must be false for a smallest n above the base case. We examine that smallest n and show that there is an even smaller n for which the statement is false. That contradictory conclusion proves that the statement is true for all n.

184. See Wikipedia "Mathematical Induction" for the colorful his-

tory of induction. Wikipedia "Peano axioms" has details about the currently accepted version.

185. Let an ocean of water represent the collection of real numbers. Imagine the volume of water corresponding to the real numbers that can be represented with a finite number of digits. It turns out that the volume is equal to 0.
One may express this fact also as follows. Randomly pick a real number. It would be a miracle if the number could be specified with a finite number of digits.

186. The mathematician L. E. J. Brouwer (1881–1966) was greatly troubled by these supposedly natural additions to mathematics. He attempted to combat them with a new theory of mathematics called *Intuitionism*. In the 1930s, Brouwer lost a huge fight with other mathematicians, in particular David Hilbert (1862–1943), about the correctness of Intuitionism. Today that concept is considered interesting, but not relevant for mathematical developments. See Wikipedia "L. E. J. Brouwer," "Intuitionism," and "Brouwer-Hilbert controversy."

187. [Truemper, 2017] assembles more than a dozen language games showing that mathematics is invented.

188. See Wikipedia "Applied mathematics" and "Pure mathematics."

189. For a breathtaking overview, see Martin Grötschel's lecture "Moderne Mathematik" ("Modern Mathematics") available at ht tps://www.youtube.com/watch?v=8RQVmn8Iqjo.

190. The cited quotes are translation of passages in [Wolchover, 2022].

Chapter 24 Immutable Neuroprocesses

191. See Wikiquote "Carl Friedrich Gauss," Gauss-Schumacher Briefwechsel, 1862.

192. See Wikipedia "Why there is anything at all" and "Existence."

193. See Wikipedia "Multiverse."

194. See Wikipedia "Metaphysics." For further details about philosophers rejecting metaphysics, see for example the Wikipedia entries "Francis Bacon," "David Hume," "Immanuel Kant," "A. J. Ayer," "Rudolf Carnap," and "Ludwig Wittgenstein."

Chapter 25 Free Will

195. See Wikipedia "Free will" and "Neuroscience of free will," as well as Stanford Encyclopedia of Philosophy "Free Will." The Stanford summary has more than 18,000 words. An Internet search of "free will" in May 2022 produced more than 15 billion results.

196. See Wikipedia "Free will."

197. See Stanford Encyclopedia of Philosophy "Free Will."

198. See Stanford Encyclopedia of Philosophy "Free Will."

199. [Truemper, 2021].

Appendix A: Two Questions

200. See [Hülster, 2019b, Hülster, 2019a] for a detailed treatment of impermissible philosophical statements.

201. Chapter 7 [Wittgenstein, 1963].

202. Paragraph 116 [Wittgenstein, 1958].

203. Preface [Wittgenstein, 1958].

Bibliography

[Abbott, 2013] Abbott, D. (2013). The reasonable ineffectiveness of mathematics. *Proceedings of the IEEE*, vol. 101.

[Augustine, 400] Augustine, Saint. (400). *Confessions*. English version by J. G. Pilkington, published 1867 in *The Early Church Fathers and Other Works*, Wm. B. Ermans Publishing Company. The original statement in Latin is, "quid est ergo tempus? si nemo ex me quaerat scio; si quaerenti explicare velim, nescio." See https://faculty.georgetown.edu/jod/latinconf/11.html.

[Barry, 2021] Barry, S. R. (2021). *Coming to Our Senses*. Basic Books.

[Beck et al., 1979] Beck, A. T., Rush, A. J., Shaw, B. F., and Emery, G. (1979). *Cognitive Therapy of Depression*. Guilford Press.

[Bennett et al., 2007] Bennett, M., Dennett, D., Hacker, P., and Searle, J. (2007). *Neuroscience and Philosophy*. Blackwell.

[Bennett and Hacker, 2003] Bennett, M. R. and Hacker, P. M. S. (2003). *Philosophical Foundations of Neuroscience*. Blackwell.

[Burns, 2008] Burns, D. D. (2008). *Feeling Good: The New Mood Therapy*. Harper.

[Burns, 2020] Burns, D. D. (2020). *Feeling Great: The Revolutionary New Treatment for Depression and Anxiety*. PESI Publishing & Media.

[Cajori, 1919] Cajori, F. (1919). *A History of the Conceptions of Limits and Fluxions in Great Britain*. Open Court Publishing Company; go to https://archive.org/index.php and search for "Limits and Fluxions Florian Cajori".

[Cantor, 1895] Cantor, G. (1895). Beiträge zur Begründung der transfiniten Mengenlehre, Erster Artikel. *Mathematische Annalen*, vol. 46, pp. 481–512.

[Conant and Ashby, 1970] Conant, R. C. and Ashby, W. R. (1970). Every good regulator of a system must be a model of that system. *International Journal of Systems Science*, vol. 1, pp. 89–97.

[Damasio, 2021] Damasio, A. (2021). *Feeling & Knowing*. Pantheon Books.

[Degenaar, 1996] Degenaar, M. (1996). *Molyneux's Problem*. Kluwer Academic Publishers; translated from the Dutch by M. J. Collins.

[Eagleman, 2020] Eagleman, D. (2020). *Livewired: The Inside Story of the Ever-Changing Brain*. Pantheon Books.

[Edgar, 2015] Edgar, S. (2015). The Physiology of the Sense Organs and Early Neo-Kantian Conceptions of Objectivity: Helmholtz, Lange, Liebmann. Chapter 6 of *Objectivity in Science*, Flavia Padovani, Alan Richardson, and Jonathan Y. Tsou (eds.), Springer Verlag.

[Einstein, 2003] Einstein, A. (2003). *The Meaning of Relativity*. Routledge; sixth edition; first edition in German and English published in 1922.

[Engel and Stäckel, 1895] Engel, F. and Stäckel, P. (1895). *Die Theorie der Parallellinien von Euklid bis auf Gauß*. Teubner Verlag; available at https://archive.org/details/theoriederparall00stac.

[Gärdenfors, 2004] Gärdenfors, P. (2004). *Conceptual Spaces: The Geometry of Thought*. MIT Press.

[Gibson et al., 2013] Gibson, A. S. C., De Koning, J. J., Thompson, K. G., Roberts, W. O., Micklewright, D., Raglin, J., and Foster, C. (2013). Crawling to the finish line: why do endurance runners collapse? Implications for understanding of mechanisms underlying pacing and fatigue. *Sports Medicine*, vol. 43, pp. 413–424.

[Gladwell, 2005] Gladwell, M. (2005). *blink: The Power of Thinking Without Thinking*. Little, Brown and Company.

[Goethe, 1810] Goethe, J. W. (1810). *Entwurf einer Farbenlehre.* English version *Goethe's Theory of Colours* available at https://ww w.gutenberg.org/ebooks/50572.

[Grafton, 2020] Grafton, S. (2020). *Physical Intelligence: The Science of How the Body and the Mind Guide Each Other Through Life.* Penguin Random House.

[Grötschel, 2020] Grötschel, M. (2020). Zeit in Natur und Kultur. *Nova Acta Leopoldina,* no. 425.

[Hacker, 2019] Hacker, P. M. S. (2019). *Wittgenstein: Meaning and Mind, Part I: Essays.* Wiley Blackwell.

[Hamming, 1980] Hamming, R. W. (1980). The unreasonable effectiveness of mathematics. *The American Mathematical Monthly,* vol. 87.

[Hawking and Mlodinow, 2010] Hawking, S. and Mlodinow, L. (2010). *The Grand Design.* Bantam Books.

[Hülster, 2019a] Hülster, F. (2019a). *Einführung in Wittgensteins Tractatus Logico-Philosophicus.* Leibniz Company.

[Hülster, 2019b] Hülster, F. (2019b). *Introduction to Wittgenstein's Tractatus Logico-Philosophicus.* Leibniz Company.

[Kabat-Zinn, 1990] Kabat-Zinn, J. (1990). *Full Catastrophe Living.* Dell Publishing.

[Kahneman, 2011] Kahneman, D. (2011). *Thinking, Fast and Slow.* Farrar, Straus, and Giroux.

[Kaku, 2021] Kaku, M. (2021). *The God Equation.* Doubleday.

[Kepler, 1627] Kepler, J. (1627). *Tabulae Rudolphinae (Rudolphine Tables).* https://archive.org/details/tabulaerudolphin00ke pl/page/n1/mode/2up. A book produced in 2014 contains the original Latin text and a German translation. It uses the fonts and graphics of the original book for both versions—an astonishing achievement. Title: *Die Rudolphinischen Tafeln.* Editor: Jürgen Reichert. Publisher: Königshausen & Neumann, 2014. See https://www.amazon.de/Die-Rudolphinischen-Tafe ln-J%C3%BCrgen-Reichert/dp/3826053524.

[Lakatos, 2015] Lakatos, I. (2015). *Proofs and Refutations*. Cambridge University Press, reissue edition.

[Livio, 2009] Livio, M. (2009). *Is God a Mathematician?* Simon & Schuster.

[Mlodinow, 2022] Mlodinow, L. (2022). *Emotional: How Feelings Shape Our Thinking*. Pantheon Books.

[Nestor, 2020] Nestor, J. (2020). *Breath: The New Science of a Lost Art*. Riverhead Books.

[Newman, 1956] Newman, J. R. (1956). *The World of Mathematics, Vols. I-IV*. Simon & Schuster; go to `https://archive.org/index.php` and search for "james newman world of mathematics".

[Oxenford, 1930] Oxenford, J. (1930). *Conversations of Goethe with Eckermann*. J. M. Dent, London. The book is a translation of J. P. Eckermann's *Gespräche mit Goethe*.

[Popper, 1992] Popper, K. R. (1992). *The Logic of Scientific Discovery*. Routledge. The original German book *Logik der Forschung* was published in 1935.

[Rudman, 2007] Rudman, P. S. (2007). *How Mathematics Happened*. Prometheus Books.

[Selinger et al., 2015] Selinger, J. C., O'Connor, S. M., Wong, J. D., and Donelan, J. M. (2015). Humans Can Continuously Optimize Energetic Cost during Walking. *Current Biology*, vol. 25, pp. 2452–2456.

[Théra, 2017] Théra, M. (2017). Homo sapiens, homo ludens. *Journal of Optimization Theory and Applications*, vol. 172.

[Truemper, 2017] Truemper, K. (2017). *The Construction of Mathematics: The Human Mind's Greatest Achievement*. Leibniz Company.

[Truemper, 2021] Truemper, K. (2021). *Magic, Error, and Terror: How Models in Our Brain Succeed and Fail*. Leibniz Company.

[Valvo, 2014] Valvo, A. (2014). *Sight Restoration After Long-term Illness: The Problems and Behavior Patterns of Visual Rehabilitation*. American Foundation for the Blind.

[Wigner, 1960] Wigner, E. P. (1960). The unreasonable effectiveness of mathematics in the natural sciences. *Communications on Pure and Applied Mathematics*, vol. 13.

[Wittgenstein, 1958] Wittgenstein, L. (1958). *Philosophical Investigations*. Basil Blackwell; available at `https://drive.google.com/file/d/0Bw-duXxYihdvWVlFaUhzclY5Vmc/edit`.

[Wittgenstein, 1963] Wittgenstein, L. (1963). *Tractatus Logico-Philosophicus*. Routledge & Kegan Paul Ltd; go to `https://people.umass.edu/klement/tlp/tlp.pdf` for the German version and two translations into English.

[Wittgenstein, 1978] Wittgenstein, L. (1978). *Remarks on Colour*. University of California Press.

[Wolchover, 2022] Wolchover, N. (2022). Wie viele reelle Zahlen gibt es? *Spektrum der Wissenschaften*, January, 2022.

[Wolfram, 2013] Wolfram, S. (2013). New Directions in the Foundations of Mathematics (2002). In *Mathematics, Computer Science, and Logic - A Never Ending Story*. P. Paule ed., Springer Verlag.

[Wolfram, 2022] Wolfram, S. (2022). The Physicalization of Metamathematics and Its Implications for the Foundations of Mathematics. https://writings.stephenwolfram.com/2022/03/.

[Zacks, 2020] Zacks, J. M. (2020). Event Perception and Memory. *Annual Review of Psychology*, vol. 71.

Acknowledgements

M. Grötschel made an extraordinary contribution with an extensive evaluation of several drafts.

Comments, technical advice, evaluation of chapters, corrections, or general help were provided by H. Elshatlawy, K. J. Friston, P. M. S. Hacker, E. Joyce, M. Opperud, T. Willmann, and S. Wolfram.

I. Truemper and U. Truemper were patient editors.

The University of Texas at Dallas—our home institution—made essential resources available.

We thank all of them for their help.

K. T.

Index